Grow Food, Cook Food, Share Food

Grow Food, Cook Food, Share Food

Perspectives on Eating from the Past and a Preliminary Agenda for the Future

KEN ALBALA

Oregon State University Press | CORVALLIS, OREGON

The paper in this book meets the guidelines for permanence and durability of the Committee on Production Guidelines for Book Longevity of the Council on Library Resources and the minimum requirements of the American National Standard for Permanence of Paper for Printed Library Materials z39.48-1984.

Library of Congress Cataloging-in-Publication Data

Albala, Ken, 1964- author.

  Grow food, cook food, share food : perspectives on eating from the past and a preliminary agenda for the future / Ken Albala.

   pages cm

  Includes bibliographical references and index.

  ISBN 978-0-87071-718-5 (alk. paper) -- ISBN 978-0-87071-719-2 (e-book)

  1. Food habits. 2. Food preferences. 3. Cooking. I. Title.

  GT2850.A53 2013

  394.1'2--dc23

                        2013013089

Oregon State University Press

121 The Valley Library

Corvallis OR 97331

541-737-3166 • fax 541-737-3170

www.osupress.oregonstate.edu

The OSU Press Horning Visiting Scholars
Publication Series

EDITORS: *Anita Guerrini and David Luft*

Previously published:

*Aetna and the Moon: Explaining Nature in Ancient Greece
and Rome*

LIBA TAUB

*Artisan/Practitioners and the Rise of the New Sciences,
1400–1600*

PAMELA O. LONG

L'ECONOMIA
DEL CITTADINO
IN VILLA
DI VINCENZO TANARA.
Libri VII.

Intitolati. Il Pane, e'l Vino. Le Viti, e l'Api. Il Cortile.
L'Horto. Il Giardino. La Terra.
La Luna, e'l Sole.

Oue con erudita varietà ſi rappreſenta, per meʒo
dell'Agricoltura, vna Vita ciuile,
e con iſparmio.

IN BOLOGNA, MDCXLIV.

CON LICENZA DE' SVPERIORI.

Courtesy, The Lilly Library, Indiana University, Bloomington, Indiana

CONTENTS

The Thomas Hart and Mary Jones Horning Endowment in the Humanities at Oregon State University was established by a bequest from Benjamin Horning (1890–1991) in memory of his parents, Mary Jones and Thomas Hart Horning, members of pioneering families of Benton County and Corvallis, Oregon. Benjamin B. Horning graduated in 1914 from what was then Oregon Agricultural College, and went on to complete a medical degree at Harvard and a degree in public health at the Johns Hopkins University. Dr. Horning's long professional career included service in public health in Connecticut, work on rural health as a staff member with the American Public Health Association, and a position as medical director for the W. K. Kellogg Foundation, which led to his spending many years in Latin America. Dr. Horning wanted his bequest at Oregon State University to expand education in the humanities and to build a bridge between the humanities and the sciences.

Since 1994, the endowment has supported an annual lecture series and individual lectures, conferences, symposia, and colloquia, as well as teaching, research, and program and library collection development. The Horning professorships are housed in the Department of History in the School of History, Philosophy, and Religion. The first Thomas Hart and Mary Jones Horning Professors in the Humanities, Mary Jo Nye and Robert A. Nye, were appointed in 1994. Anita Guerrini and David A. Luft succeeded them in 2008. The Horning Visiting Scholar in the Humanities program was inaugurated in 2006 to allow a distinguished scholar to spend a week in residence at OSU and deliver a series of lectures as well as participate in other activities in and out of the classroom. Visiting Scholars have included Liba

Taub (Cambridge University), John Beatty (University of British Columbia), and Pamela O. Long (independent scholar).

The OSU Press Horning Visiting Scholars Publication Series, under the direction of the Press's acquisitions editor, Mary Elizabeth Braun, publishes the public lectures delivered by the Horning Visiting Scholar: two volumes in the series have appeared, Liba Taub's *Aetna and the Moon* (2008) and Pamela O. Long's *Artisan/Practitioners and the New Science* (2011). Other works in the humanities outside the scope of this series that the series editors have found to be relevant to the aims of the Horning Endowment may also be published by the Press in the future. Ken Albala was the Horning Visiting Scholar in November 2011. Dr. Albala, Professor of History at Pacific University in Stockton, California, is a well-known historian of food. His research and scholarship have focused particularly on the Renaissance but have ranged widely to include two recent books written with Rosanna Nafziger on traditional food and household skills, *The Lost Art of Real Cooking* (2010) and *The Lost Arts of Hearth and Home* (2012). Other titles among his ten books include *Eating Right in the Renaissance* (2002); *Beans: A History* (2007), winner of the 2008 International Association of Culinary Professionals Jane Grigson Award and the Cordon d'Or in Food History/Literature; and most recently *Three World Cuisines: Italian, Mexican, Chinese* (2012), which won the 2013 Gourmand World Cookbook Award for "Best Foreign Cuisine Book in the World." Until recently he co-edited the scholarly journal *Food, Culture and Society*, and he is general editor of the *AltaMira Studies in Food and Gastronomy* (Rowman & Littlefield).

In *Grow Food, Cook Food, Share Food*, Ken Albala offers, as his subtitle states, "perspectives on eating from the past and a preliminary agenda for the future." Drawing on his vast knowledge of preindustrial food production and consumption, he offers a concise and personal account of how we might regain some of the lost pleasures of past food practices. As any reader of his *Lost Arts* books or his blog ("Ken Albala's Food Rant") knows, Dr. Albala practices what he preaches.

He begins his story with his own childhood in what was then rural New Jersey, moving on to see what we can learn from ancient, medieval, and early modern Italian agricultural manuals, each of which offers a different model of agrarian life and its relationship to the city. Just as modern urbanites—that is, most Americans—have lost touch with where our food comes from, so too we have lost touch with how to prepare it. Employing fermentation as displayed in the making of bread, salami, and cheese, Dr. Albala takes us through the process of making these foods as they had been made for thousands of years. The third part of this equation, and perhaps the most important, is sharing food with others. Exploring the role of food in family, religion, and ritual, he shows how food builds community and indeed, human happiness.

Albala is not sentimental about the past, and his aim in this book is not to evoke nostalgia but to provoke us to action. *Grow Food, Cook Food, Eat Food* is a delightful polemic that will make you want to grow your own grapes and make your own cheese, and consume them with friends and family.

Anita Guerrini

THE APPETIZER

I would like to thank all the marvelous people I met during a perfectly delightful week in Corvallis in the fall of 2011 while delivering the lectures that were the basis of this little book. Above all, thanks to Anita Guerrini who arranged everything and even let me mess up her kitchen. Thanks to the late Benjamin B. Horning whose munificence made the trip possible. Thanks also to Joan Gross, Sara Jameson, Mary Jo and Bob Nye, Flo Leibowitz, Jon Katz, and all the fantastic students and people from the community who prompted me with thoughtful questions. Thanks also to Allen Goodman and Hilarie Phelps at the Harrison House. I never suspected a stay at a B&B would include great conversations over breakfast. Thanks to Laura McCandlish with whom I took a fabulous tour of the 2 Towns Ciderhouse. And thanks to all the lovely people who shared food with me or provided great ingredients at the farmer's market. A big thanks to all the people at Oregon State University Press who turned this into a book, especially Mary Braun and copy editor Julie Talbot.

The lectures on which this book is based are partly drawn from my research as a food historian, but also from my personal experience growing, cooking, and sharing food. Whenever people ask me why I spend so much time cooking and writing cookbooks, I tell them this is the activist phase of my career. As you will see herein, I believe that practice of history, while valuable in and of itself, should also engage the public and inspire people to generate social change. In my small way, these ruminations on the garden, kitchen, and dining room are designed to do just that. I hope you can follow me and get your hands a little dirty.

In these lectures I discuss the historical development of three crucial components of human nourishment and their disjuncture in the industrial era. I have tried to describe without romantic sentimentality the ways our food production system, our methods of food preparation, and our modes of consumption have changed over time to the detriment of human happiness, health, and community. I have also made some creative suggestions regarding ways in which we can recapture the positive aspects of past foodways without endangering food security or abandoning the many valuable advances of the last century. History offers constructive examples of how we can better grow food, cook food, and share it, if only we have the means to listen and learn from food writers of the past.

KEN ALBALA

Grow Food, Cook Food, Share Food

Wellcome Library, London

Grow Food

There is a certain magic to watching little shoots nudging their way up through the soil, spreading their first leaves and soaking up sunshine and water. I think at some level, at least for the past 10,000 years, we have evolved so closely with domesticated plants and animals that it makes us happy to just observe their fecundity. There is also something so rewarding when the yield from your labor in the field can be harvested directly to provide nourishment for yourself and others. Even just wandering through gardens and orchards sown by others gives us a palpable feeling of wellbeing. Farming and processing food are an inherent part of what it means to be human, yet so many of us in the last century have lost contact with the soil and have completely forgotten how to prepare basic raw ingredients for storage. Growing and preserving food have always been two sides of the same process. Beans and fruits were dried, vegetables were pickled, milk was transformed into cheese, and meat was cured right on the farm. Yet since the advent of industrial food production, the farm has become completely detached from the food factory, and basic knowledge not only of how our food is grown but how it is processed has been lost. This is partly due to the scale of today's farming and food processing operations, but it also has to do with the physical space we occupy and our relationship to the land.

When I was very young, my family moved from Brooklyn to the township of Manalapan in central New Jersey. For my parents this was the equivalent of moving out to the country. Although we lived in a new, mass-produced housing development built by

Levitt (the company that effectively invented suburban planning), the area was still almost completely rural. It was 1966, and you could hear cows mooing early in the morning. My friends and I used to walk to nearby cornfields, by late summer towering maybe seven or eight feet high. We would scatter, dashing through the rows, our arms being scratched by wayward leaves, until we were dizzy and lost. Most importantly, there were produce stands that sold vegetables, including tomatoes of unspeakably intense flavor and beauty. In these days the term "Garden State" was not facetious in the least. We were surrounded by farms, and at the time there still stood many old farmhouses.[1] The area was settled in the 1680s by Scots and Quakers and a mile away there was the old, spooky Topanemus Cemetery set in a patch of woods where we would visit the old farmers' graves, families like the Barriclos and Reeds, and muse upon the weathered headstones with their gruesome skull and crossbones motifs and macabre rhymes. "As I once was, so you shall be, so prepare for death and follow me."[2]

From the time these first settlers arrived until about the 1960s, for nearly three hundred years, the principal economic base of the region was agriculture. This was not subsistence agriculture, nor even production of fruits and vegetables for the local market. These were fairly large farms supplying processed ingredients to the cities. The grain grown here was milled and shipped to New York or Philadelphia in the form of flour; the apple orchards all through the area processed fruit into alcohol known as applejack.[3] Laird & Company, started nearby, has been in business since the eighteenth century and is the last surviving producer of applejack. By the 1830s, food was transported by cart or canal to the Raritan River, the Hudson or the Delaware. By the time my family had moved there, only the names remained of the many mills that straddled the network of streams: Taylor's Mills Road; Lafayette Mills School, which was a few hundred feet from my house; and Clark Mills, where I went to kindergarten.

Within a decade of our moving there, the housing developments began to proliferate. We had no right to complain, we were merely the first trickle of what would eventually become a deluge of houses, making up bedroom communities that stretched without break from Boston to Washington, D.C. If you visit the area today, there are still a few green patches, preserved as state parks, like the site of the Battle of Monmouth in 1778, and the odd little remnants of what was once extensive farmland. But now it is mostly houses, strip malls, and business complexes. The showroom on Route 9 that once sold John Deere tractors now carries lawn mowers. Remnants of the little cemetery are still there, but now surrounded by housing developments, the old dirt path long ago paved for traffic. This is a story replicated through much of the country, and there is no point in being nostalgic about it. Populations rise, cities sprawl, suburbia engulfs everything in its path. Communities like these were a fascinating social experiment, but when people of my generation grew up and began to notice the wider world, we were indeed "sprung from cages on Highway 9" as local Bruce Springsteen put it. Most fled suburbia and the soulless commuter's life it engendered. In any case, it was no longer a place to farm.

Agriculture itself has profoundly changed in these years, too, not merely in becoming mechanized. Wheat production has moved to huge industrial farms in the Midwest. The applejack is made from neutral grain spirits, flavored with a little apple shipped in from Virginia. The vegetables, like those tomatoes, are now available year-round, picked green, gassed, and shipped all around the country. They are now a little rounder, harder, a brighter shade of red, but not tasting much of anything. This, too, was perhaps not inevitable, but it has already happened and it is impossible to turn back the clock.

It is still worthwhile to consider what we have lost in this process, now that the food we eat is grown by less than two percent of the population. What are the consequences of losing a direct connection to the soil and, if not growing food ourselves, then at least knowing the people who did, and having a direct concern for their personal welfare as members of the community?

Not that these connections are completely severed everywhere in the country—I am fortunate to live now in Stockton, California, in the center of the great Central Valley. It is a city surrounded by vineyards, almond groves, dairies, and every imaginable type of farm, from small family operations with farm stands to some of the biggest industrial agribusinesses on earth—the very ones that grow those hard, flavorless tomatoes. I am not merely arguing for the relative merits of small family operations over big factory farms, but for the human connection to growing food and caring for animals, and the sense of responsibility that familiarity breeds, as well as the now-severed connections that once linked cities directly to the countryside.

There are many good reasons to be optimistic nowadays. I need not recount the success of farmers' markets, Community Supported Agriculture (CSA) that delivers produce in boxes straight from the farm (cutting out middlemen), school and home gardening, and urban farms, or even the brave efforts to localize the food supply. These are all entirely laudable, even though they may make up only a small percentage of total production in the United States. There is still something missing from these efforts, something we have lost with modern food production. These things are all positive and forward looking, but I think we might also learn something invaluable through a serious glance backward, by gleaning lessons from agronomic texts of the past. What attitudes did farmers years ago apply to their efforts? What sense of wonder did they express at the fertility of the earth, and with what kind of respect did they tend to cooking and serving food that issued from their efforts?

I began with the story about the growth of suburbia to suggest that its modern version is essentially just an extension of the city.

It encroaches upon the rural landscape, devours it, but has no real synergistic connection to it, apart from the few surviving farm stands, farmers' markets that bring in produce, or the backyard gardens that people tend. I could say much the same even about where I live now; although it is an urban area with farms just beyond the city limits, the vast majority of produce from those farms is shipped elsewhere or sent to factories to be canned. The wealthier farmers and even some farm workers may live in the city, but the rural and urban are otherwise two entirely distinct and disconnected spheres. You might meet a farmer at the market and buy his tomatoes, but there is no direct economic incentive for the city dwellers to be concerned with his welfare. They can always get tomatoes elsewhere. There might be a good reason to reconsider the entire way we think about food production, to restore this direct connection to the earth and its produce, rather than merely act as consumers.

There once existed agronomic models that were radically different from modern systems. These were biologically diversified, equipped to process ingredients *in situ*, and most importantly, they were connected directly to cities. These bygone arrangements offer some lessons, even if we would not want to implement them entirely today. They come from Italy, and flourished from ancient times through the seventeenth century. Different forms of farm operations are described by three agronomists in particular: Cato the Elder (234-149 BCE), a Roman statesman; Pietro de' Crescenzi, a retired lawyer from Bologna writing in the time around 1304-1309; and Vincenzo Tanara, a Bolognese nobleman writing in the seventeenth century.[4] Each composed an extensive treatise on agriculture, the first two being classic, the latter less well known.

To get a sense of how these systems worked, let's take a look at the unique features of Italian landholding. Historically, Italy was largely urban, especially in the north, but the majority of cities were relatively small. Each city dominated the surrounding *contado*, or countryside, even ruling it politically, and the majority of land was owned by people living in the cities. There was feudalism in the Middle Ages, but it was never as important in Italy as elsewhere in Europe. Even in Roman times, large estates or *latifundia*, although prevalent elsewhere in the empire, were atypical in Italy in the Republican period. Cities were by and large fed by a surrounding rural ring of about fifty miles, or as we might say today, they were *locavore* in a very real sense. That is not to say some products such as wine, oil, and cheese didn't travel farther, they did. But most produce and domestic animals came from within a day's journey and most localities had their own distinctive ways of making bread, cheese, and salami based on their own unique, local microflora. These products were for the most part consumed locally.

There were also several different arrangements whereby land was farmed. Wealthy people would own "suburban" villas outright and hire a farmer/steward as well as farmhands on a permanent or seasonal basis. In classical times, slaves were also common, although there were usually just a handful on each estate. Large numbers such as we might imagine on a plantation were unusual. But practically anyone running an urban household would also own land as the most stable form of investment. In the Middle Ages and Renaissance this land was often farmed by the system of *mezzadria*, which is something like sharecropping. A farmer would occupy and work the land and would keep 50 percent of the produce. The other 50 percent would be sent to the owner for his own household use or to sell within the city. As you can see, the owner therefore would take an active interest in the success of the farm, often investing in improvements and/or fertilizer or drainage projects, or testing new plants and animals. This explains the prevalence of farming manuals, written for people who needed to learn how to farm in order to maximize yields and profits.[5] If the farm failed to flourish, the owner lost his investment.

Incidentally, the system also existed in Southern France, and was called *metayage*; similar systems elsewhere in Southern Europe were also used. In Italy it lasted well into the twentieth century, until officially outlawed in 1982 when all holdings were legally transformed into rental properties. There are historical reasons why it ceased to work—having largely to do with industry, cities growing too big, and agriculture itself becoming mechanized and bigger—but a closer look at the historical use of the *mezzadria* system will reveal some of its merits. It should be noted that the heyday of the system was in the wake of the bubonic plague, after 1348, when labor was at a premium and landowners offered good deals to farmers to keep them on the land.[6] The model does not work as well with overpopulation in the countryside, when landholdings tend to be divided up into tiny parcels, which is why it did not work in the nineteenth and twentieth centuries.

I am certainly not suggesting a revival of the system, or of classical villas manned by slaves! But there is something about the very close connection between countryside and city that deserves notice, something about the active interest of individuals living in the city for the welfare of the countryside, both an aesthetic and commercial interest, that we have largely lost. In all the authors discussed here, there is a sense of pride in ownership and care, which 98 percent of our current population can only experience by having their own garden or allotment—an undertaking that is almost never a commercial venture. Gardening is usually a hobby, restricted mostly to vegetables and fruit. That is to say, I think the possibility of material profit makes a person think very differently about the land. It also provides incentive to care about the farmer, in a way that an absentee landlord taking feudal dues or rents would not.

Modern consumers rarely if ever experience such a direct connection, mostly because food passes through the hands of so many middlemen. We know practically nothing about where food comes from. You might argue that Community Supported Agriculture, with the box of produce delivered to your door, approaches the connection I'm talking about, but since people can join or leave anytime and they don't own the farm or even visit (they just pay a fee), the direct investment is missing. Moreover, as with the farmer at the market, if the venture fails, people can get produce elsewhere.

Cato the Elder, even though he was not describing the *mezzadria* system, in many ways describes a similar arrangement. Without doubt, this kind of aesthetic appreciation for agriculture has its roots in the classical authors, not just Cato but others such as Virgil, Varro, Columella, and Palladius. For the Romans, getting your hands dirty, so to speak, was not in any way demeaning, in fact quite the opposite. Virgil talks about planting trees with his own hands, and wrote a long poem, the *Georgics*, about rural life. Nor were these just aristocrats playing around with gardening; farming was a commercial venture for them.

Cato the Elder is best known as the statesman who would get up onto the rostrum in the Senate and bang on it, proclaiming, "*Carthago delenda est!*" ("Carthage must be destroyed!") regardless of the topic at hand. He is also the author of the earliest surviving prose work in Latin, *De Re Agricultura*. To future generations he would be associated with the stern self-sufficient values of the Republican period, when Romans used to go off fighting in one season and then return to their farms to plow or harvest, before Rome went soft with exotic eastern luxuries. This was imagined to be a time when Romans had simple tastes, still feared the gods, and lived on small subsistence farms.

In point of fact, this description takes his work out of context. Cato was writing about farming as an investment, for men who might have just come into an inheritance, or were perhaps retired from the military and earning a pension (after ten years for equestrians, twenty years for infantry)—so someone perhaps around thirty or thirty-five years old. The text was written for anyone looking for a sound investment in land, which meant direct, if absentee, management. This was at a time when the early empire was expanding, cities were growing or being founded, and there was a lot of money to be made in trade, but especially in agriculture, thanks to great demand for food. Cato focuses on high priced goods that ship well, especially wine and oil. But the book gives directions for much more than that, especially fruits and vegetables for market gardening. Cato is adamant that you have to buy land on a major river or road system, so clearly this is food to be sold in cities. He recommends 150 acres for an olive orchard, 62 acres for a vineyard.

Importantly, these were not huge *latifundia* (plantations) growing hundreds of acres of wheat. There were not large teams of slaves. In fact, he says a good olive farm would have only thirteen slaves, six just to deal with livestock—three to drive oxen, one to tend the donkey, a swineherd, and a shepherd. The sheep grazed among the olive trees. A vineyard would need sixteen slaves for more varied tasks—like cutting willow staves for trellises or baskets. There would also be farmers, as well as slaves, who grew food to consume on site and fodder for the draught animals. But all the heavy work was contracted labor, essentially migrants brought in seasonally who worked for wages.

Overseeing the whole operation, there would have been one family, a foreman and his wife in charge of everything, following the directions given by the owner, who was usually absentee. That is, the owner stayed in the city and the foreman or steward sent the produce and processed food back to him in the city, where he used some in his household and sold the rest to merchants. This would be not just wine and oil, but vegetables and fruit, grains, cured meat and cheese—anything produced on the farm. It was different from the *mezzadria* system because the foreman was paid, rather than taking some of the produce, but note the close connection between the city and the countryside. Most importantly, the owner needed to know at all times what was going on. He was ultimately making the decisions and ideally visiting the farm as often as possible. If something went wrong he lost money, so he had to know in intimate detail the workings of the farm, the soil quality, everything. Note how different this was from a completely absentee landlord who collected rents and had little interest in what crops were grown or the technologies applied.

Cato's book is also extraordinarily detailed about how to build the farmhouses, presses, and other equipment; when to plant; and what kind of soil is best for which crops. Cato clearly knew how to farm from direct experience. Wine was made right on site and he explains how to correct its faults. There is even a culinary section where he offers recipes for sacrificial cakes, including *globi*, which are essentially fried donuts soaked in honey and rolled in poppy seeds, and *encytum*, which is a kind of funnel cake. The most interesting is called *placenta*, which is a flat cake made with layers of oiled dough, fresh cheese, and honey—sort of a sweet lasagna, without the tomatoes. Self-sufficiency was among the most cherished values among Roman agronomists, so it would not be unthinkable to have every ingredient coming from the farm, or being sourced locally.

In any case, Cato's operation provides an example of one form of agriculture that is heavily diversified, involved not only in growing but processing foodstuffs, and which directly links the countryside to the city, without middlemen or go-betweens, without the disjuncture of essential knowledge about how the food is grown, and, significantly, with a financial incentive to maintain the best practices which will make a profit. These are the crucial elements connecting city dwellers with the countryside, and from which we might learn some valuable lessons.

Imagine an arrangement today, something comparable to Cato's farm but practical for modern urbanites. Obviously there are not many people who can afford to buy hundred-acre plots of land, nor many who have the time or expertise to manage an operation like this. But consider if a group of people collectively invested in a farm, both land and equipment, and owned it jointly much like a stock company, so investors could sell their portion if they wanted to. These owners would collectively hire a farmer to live there and manage the property rent-free, but they would decide what should be grown. They would plant vegetables or have animals reared for their own personal use. The farmer would get to keep half the produce for his use. Anything left over could be sold, invested back into the farm for operating costs, upkeep, etc. On the one hand this would open opportunities for small family farms and all the burden of debt would not be on the head of the farmer. Nor would the farmer need to borrow from banks and have his debt repayment subject to the fluctuations of food prices on the open market. More importantly, it would connect people living in cities directly to the land, not as consumers, but as owners taking a personal stake in the property—in whose self-interest it would be to use the best practices. Sustainability would be requisite, not merely a marketing ploy. Ultimately, this would be both a moneymaking venture and a way to feed the investors' and farmer's families.

Today there are legal arrangements similar to this in land trusts, which historically have been used to hide ownership, though increasingly are used for conservation efforts.[7] They could also be used for active farming ventures, wherein a cohort of investors allowed a resident farmer to use the land without the burden of rent or lease, and the product of the land could be shared in kind or sold directly to the community by the farmer. Cooperative arrangements would allow the owners to take part in routine tasks simply for pleasure. This would also be quite different from community gardens, wherein people are given their own little patches, but frequently drop out or leave the work to be done by others. With the cooperative model, the profit motive provides incentive to grow fresh produce, but also value-added processed foods like cheese, cured meat, preserves, and pickles—something you almost never see in community farms today due to general loss of knowledge about how to process food, as well as complex food safety regulations that favor industrial processing.

There are other possible models drawn from the past. Let us move forward to the fourteenth century and Pietro de' Crescenzi. Pietro was not a nobleman, but a successful lawyer working at the University of Bologna. Apparently he had traveled a lot, and observed farming practices wherever he went. When he retired he decided to move to a villa outside the city walls. This was the Villa Olmo, near Rubizzano, about ten miles from Bologna, which is still farmland. There he started farming and writing a book on agriculture, based in part on classical sources, but also with much new material drawn from practical experience. His book *Opus Ruralium Commodorum* (Work on the Benefits of Rural Life) circulated in manuscript for two centuries and was then among the first books ever printed, in 1471, and was immediately translated into Italian, French, and German. It became one of the most influential books on agriculture ever written.

Crescenzi's basic attitude toward farming bears scrutiny. He did not move to the country to retire and live in leisure. He considered it a good, safe investment for an urbanite and something ennobling. In the prologue, he says among all the things that can be acquired (i.e. material goods) nothing is better than agriculture (i.e. cultivated land). Nothing is more abundant (profitable), nothing sweeter, and nothing more worthy of a free man. It is a kind of appreciation for farming that had not been seen since classical times, and certainly not from a scholar. This attitude, incidentally, should be contrasted with the standard position of feudal nobility, which was essentially as absentee landlords, letting peasants do whatever they liked with the land—mostly subsistence farming, living from hand to mouth. Crescenzi's operation was much more closely tied to the markets inside the city, and not surprisingly, he mostly discusses intensive crops like grapes, olives, fruits, and vegetables—items that can be processed and sold.

Moreover, he did not merely plant gardens and enjoy them for their own sake. This was meant to be a profitable venture; hence he invested in a wide range of improvements. Crescenzi was particularly interested in what we would call soil conservation—building canals and gullies, or leveling terraces on hills to prevent runoff. He also explained the logic of leaving stubble through the summer to prevent wind from blowing away topsoil. He reintroduced crop rotation systems, green manure, and fertilizers that would build up soil quality. He is especially lucid about lupines, which serve as cattle fodder, and as we know today, put nitrogen back into the soil. They serve the same function as alfalfa, both being legumes. The stalks of the plant can also be plowed back into the soil after harvesting, serving as green manure. Crescenzi also advocated composting and soil improvements. For marshy land he introduced rice cultivation, a completely new crop in Italy at the time, introduced from the East and through Muslim Spain.

I think Crescenzi's direct aesthetic descendants are those urbanites today who leave their jobs to work a farm, perhaps using organic methods, experimenting with new crops and irrigation techniques. He was forward thinking in the same way as the modern back-to-the-land movement. In this respect, I think he provides another model for how cities can be linked to the countryside; that is, directly—by enterprising individuals who want to cultivate land themselves in new ways, for profit. Interestingly, Crescenzi is also health conscious; he describes the medicinal virtues of both wild and sown plants. He even offers some basic recipes for products like verjuice (the juice of unripe grapes) and vinegar, both means of preserving grape juice as condiments.

Most significantly, there is an aesthetic appreciation for farming, much like you find in Barbara Kingsolver or Wendell Berry. These are educated city people taking a direct interest in farming their own land, learning about the soil qualities and the best crops to grow, and doing it as a personal source of food and income, not merely for entertainment. The profit incentive makes this quite different from a hobby farm. Of course, there are some modern urbanites who start their own operations, have to make a profit, and certainly bring a deep appreciation for rural life. This may be the future of farming, or at least we will see scattered farms like this amidst the factory farms. But there can certainly be more, and not merely among the few who opt for a complete lifestyle overhaul, but for those of us who want to keep our day jobs and also want more than a handshake at the farmer's market, a box dropped at the doorstep, or the occasional agritourism vacation.

The last example is Vincenzo Tanara, also from Bologna, who in 1644 wrote *L'economica del cittadino in Villa* (The Economy or Management of the City Dweller in the Villa). Like Crescenzi's work, it is specifically written for city people connected to the countryside. Tanara however was a nobleman, a Marchese, who had inherited some land and was given more for his military prowess. But unlike his fellow nobles, his book is all about how to turn the best profit by direct cultivation and processing everything yourself to maximize returns, which is why the book is filled with recipes, too—ones he had definitely made himself and shared. Tanara is a kind of do-it-yourself enthusiast about everything that can be made on his villa.

For example, immediately after discussing water quality he goes directly into a recipe for making beer, drawn from his own experience. He describes soaking the barley for twenty-four hours and preparing the leavening. When the barley begins to germinate and swell, it is malted, broken up, mixed with hot water (just hot enough to put one's hand in). Then hops are added. He describes the equipment and terminology, different additives people used. The instructions are similar to any beer-making recipe you would find today, although he was starting entirely with raw ingredients. There are also extraordinarily detailed bread-making instructions, all the way from calculating the price of wheat per pound, to milling, bolting, making and keeping the leavening, baking in an oven, and various types of bread. There are also bread recipes including a soup called *lova* made with broth and grated *Parmigiano*, garnished with marrow, testicles, little livers, and cock's combs (the squishy red things on roosters' heads)—or with chicken or turkey and slices of cheese to make a *capirotata*—all sprinkled with sugar and cinnamon. Tanara had very Baroque tastes, hence the use of exotic garnishes, including musk and ambergris. He was not entirely self-sufficient; there were certainly luxuries like spices that he purchased, but nearly everything else came directly from his own farm.

Tanara seems to have really enjoyed the connection between growing the ingredients and transforming them into the best products possible; it was all about superior quality and taste for him, and that comes from knowing how to make everything yourself. When he is done discussing a procedure, there are usually a few paragraphs in praise of bread or wine, or whatever food he is creating. Not only is there detailed discussion of how to make wine, but of how to tend the vines and trellis them, and when to harvest. He also covers other products created from grapes, like verjuice, made from unripe grapes in July, and *sapa*, which is a sweetener made of grape must boiled down to a third of its volume. There are directions on how to make vinegar and various grape sauces such as *sapori*, something like a grape jelly, but served with meat. There is a *salsa verde* made from the sour vine tendrils. His is a mostly self-sufficient household that uses every available ingredient to some useful purpose. Tanara's work is among the very few that take you all the way from growing the food to preserving it, cooking it, and serving it.

The diversification of this farm is very impressive. Anything and everything that can be raised or grown is found here, so you not only have vines and bees, but cows for dairy products, chickens, pig sties, a dovecote, herbs for seasoning, a vegetable garden, fruit trees, and medicine. The way all these activities fit together Tanara calls the economy of the household, and he uses the term in every sense, meaning being frugal, avoiding stinginess or avarice, but also generous with your bounty. As well, every part of the farm contributes to something else. The manure from animals is used as fertilizer. The pigs feed on vegetable waste and the entire operation works as a unified system without external inputs. It functions as a whole economy, so to speak. But it is also connected to the city, because the extra produce of the entire operation is sold there.

Economy here also means not wasting anything. There is a section on bovine butchery where Tanara describes which parts are good for broth, which should be roasted or stewed, and the prized status of brains, fat, marrow, and spleen. Everything gets used in one way or another. And anything left after goes into meatballs. He says, "Between the economist and the cook, there is little discord over meatballs, which are also for the most part cooked in a pot, the cook calls meatballs the queen of dishes, because with these he can satisfy every taste, using a diversity of ingredients, equally the economist, who gets a great piece of meat with what is removed from the bones, nerves, skin, etc."[8] And then he describes how these extra parts are mixed with *ricotta*, grated *Parmigiano*, parsley, garlic, raisins, spices, eggs, salt, bread soaked in broth, a little verjuice, all cut up very finely or pounded in a mortar, and lightly fried. Then he prefers cooking them in a covered pot in the oven overnight or on hot coals to make the meatballs as tender as possible. In any case, he is using every part of the animal economically and in the interest of taste.

Tanara's true passion, however, is pork; in this section he describes 110 different foods to make from pork, using every imaginable part, from head to tail and every single bit in between. Nothing goes to waste. He starts anatomically with the eyes and snout, which are good simmered and cured in salt; sliced and topped with oil, vinegar, pepper, and coriander; and served as a salad. One can imagine the slices of snout looking like buttons on a plate. Every piece has uses—the fat and feet in gelatin; the blood in sausages and pies; the skin, tripe and nerves in soup; everything else goes into sausages and salami. Or, he suggests, prepare pork as the poor do, taking the heart, skin, eyes, snout, kidneys, and fat, and pounding everything together with salt, pepper, and fennel, then stuffing everything into a stomach and letting it dry. Tanara next, in good comedic form, describes the pig's last will and testament. His bristles he leaves to painters to make little brushes; half his skin goes to sculptors to make stucco, the other half to make soap; his fat is proffered to make candles for people to read by; his bones are left to comedians (presumably for slapsticks); his nails to gardeners to grow carrots; and all other parts—lardo, prosciutto, ribs, belly, salami, mortadella, sausages—to *il carissimo Economo villeggiante* (our most dear rural economical householder).[9]

About cheese making at his villa, Tanara definitely speaks from personal experience and I think exemplifies the model of engaged landowner-artisan. He starts with consideration of the milk, positing that cow's milk is best because the heavy part, the viscous part, and the watery part are all in equal measure. Cow's milk is especially good in the spring when the animals are feeding on a variety of herbs whose medicinal virtues are transmitted directly into the cheese. By comparison, sheep's milk has too little whey and goat's milk too little butter, or fat, so it is not as good for health. But in terms of taste, he admits, people say just the opposite. A common saying ran, *Si lac dulce sapit subito cur putret? Aquosum est.* (If milk tastes sweet, why does it spoil quickly? Because it's watery.) Furthermore, *Quod praestat? Capra post, ovis inde, bovis.* (Which is best? First goat, then sheep, then cow.)[10]

Tanara has definitely made cheese with his own hands as well. He says it is best to break up the curds with one's hands into small pieces, place them in a vessel, then lift up the solid parts with both hands and press gently, so the watery serum drips down. Next, place it in a *forma* (mold) of wood. If unsalted, this makes *lattarolo*; if half-salted, a cheese called *tenero*; if fat and buttery, it's *ravaglioso* in Rome but *tomino* in Bologna. If then aged, it becomes especially useful for people like voyagers and warriors, because it is extremely nourishing—whence comes *Si caseum haberem, non desideratam obsonium.* (If you've had cheese, you don't need anything else to go with bread.) Such aged cheese is harmful for the leisurely, students, and convalescents (because it is difficult to digest); nonetheless, everything is more tasty when such cheese is grated on top.

Tanara clearly prefers the taste criteria over that of health, and continues to praise aged cheese: "*Quest'è una delle tre cose, che mondo vecchissime sono buone, l'oglio il caccio, & il conseglio.*" ("This is one of three things that are better the older they are: oil, cheese, and advice.") His personal favorites appear to be cheeses from Lodi, which weigh up to 400 pounds. But *marzolino* made in the Tuscan hills is also very fine, and he even makes a concession to the Apennine hills south of Parma. Tanara is also explicit about the many ways to preserve cheese: it can be smoked, soaked in brine, or rubbed with fat and dusted with rice flour. But he really waxes rhapsodic when he talks about ways to serve cheese. He says *Parmigiano* and *Lodegiana* are to be cut in the thinnest slices, placed in a dish, and drizzled with oil and the juice of oranges or lemon, then placed over a fire until a crust is formed. This is then scraped directly onto bread. *Tomino* can be cooked on a spit. But the apotheosis of cheese is in fillings for ravioli, anolini, or tortelli, with aromatic flavorings such as pistachios, pine nuts, raisins, jujubes, candied citrus peel, cherries, gooseberries, pea puree, or cock's combs and testicles. Better yet, truffles and grated prosciutto. These sound a little strange, but they are precisely the ingredients called for in Bartolomeo Stefani's *L'arte di ben cucinare* (The Art of Fine Cooking). Stefani worked for the Gonzaga in

Mantua but he was Bolognese and a contemporary of Tanara. I would not be surprised if the nobleman had eaten these dishes prepared by the chef himself.

The following recipe, Stefani's *Torta di Formaggio Fresco*, will give an excellent idea of the aesthetic of the era. It is the epitome of Baroque cuisine.

Take three pounds of cheese and pound in a mortar, making sure it's fat enough, and add a pound and a half of rich ricotta, a pound of pine nuts that have been soaked in rose water, and pound everything together. Add a pound of cream, 10 egg yolks, half ounce of cinnamon and 6 ounces of sugar, mix everything well, make a fine pastry leaf, and a pan of the right size buttered, and place on the leaf, then the composition and cook it in an oven . . . It's served hot with sugar on top.[11]

Tanara is no less enthusiastic about gardening. He says a villa without a garden is like a body without a soul. It provides the salad greens, aromatics, medicinal herbs, fruits, vegetables, and flowers for pleasure. At one point he describes planting beans, letting them run over a pergola, or on a cane frame.[12] When they are still young in the pod, he says to put them in a salad with honeyed vinegar and pepper—or parboil and flour them, then fry and serve with a garlic sauce. Young, freshly shelled beans are fried in a pan with garlic and onions, parsley, mint, and *sapa*. Or once they're mature and dry, put the beans into a soup for Lent. There is a kind of excitement and delight over growing and preparing food in Tanara's writing that's infectious. He makes you want to grow and process your own food.

The most important characteristics of all three agronomists is that they are discussing a relatively small-scale and diversified farm rather than one that is specialized or monoculture; one that serves a nearby city, that is operated as an investment, and that supports a family and a variety of workers. Even though the land is held differently in each case, it is owned by someone whose primary profession is not farming. It seems obvious that the lesson to be drawn from all three cases is that people should not be fundamentally ignorant of where food comes from. Two percent of the population should not be growing sustenance for the rest, and there should be more formal ways of getting people involved in food production and processing, beyond backyard gardening or buying from local farmers.

The farming cooperative would be the closest modern equivalent of these historic examples. This would be a farm where one comes and works on the farm for a set length of time and takes home produce equal to the share of labor put in. This idea occurred to me recently as I was helping a friend with a manual wine pressing—using a big, wood-slatted press with a huge screw and crossbar on top. Four or five men and one woman worked one long morning to press about ten barrels of wine, and we each took home a case of a previous batch. Any one of us could have gone and bought a case of good local wine for maybe $150. For five hours of labor, thirty dollars an hour is actually very good pay. But no one even thought about time or money, because money was not involved at any stage. Yet in one morning I learned how to press grapes with technology no different than was used a thousand years ago, and it was remarkably enjoyable work and bore no resemblance whatsoever to industrial wine production. I cannot honestly say I would feel the same way baling hay or cleaning chicken coops, but I would certainly give it a try if I got to take home a few chickens. That is, the exchange of labor for payment in kind seems so far from our modern agronomic sensibilities, that it should be explored as a systematic option.

There are, of course, agritourism sites that work in comparable ways, but I am thinking of this as a year-round commitment to a farm near where you live, rather than on vacation in Tuscany. You would agree to work a few hours a week on a farm, and you take home a proportion of whatever you do. Obviously there would need to be practical adjustments—heavy farm machinery is not something most people can operate—but perhaps such machinery is not necessary when producing on diversified farms where there are many small tasks that are artisanal processes rather than huge, industrial-scale operations.

Here is another example: Just south of where I live there are miles and miles of almond orchards. I brought a group of students to one orchard during harvest season, and it was very frightening. They have a tiny truck that grabs the tree and shakes it violently so all the almonds fall off. (I was told it's why they pronounce them "ah-monds," because the machine shakes the "l" out of them.) There's a different truck that scoops everything into windrows, and yet another that collects them. Then a huge machine the size of a house removes the dirt and sticks; we were told it costs several hundred thousand dollars a year to operate, just in electricity. Another machine dehusks, shells, and pasteurizes the almonds to remove possible *salmonella, E. coli,* or other pathogens that might have been in the dirt. It occurred to everyone in the class that you could just pick the almonds and put them in a bag, which is exactly how it used to be done (with migrant labor, admittedly). The machines are clearly the only way to do this efficiently now, because of the enormous scale of the operation and the fact that they are supplying a world market. Notice how the nature of this business and its sheer size dictate mechanical measures that have almost completely removed humans from the picture, even introducing extraordinary processing such as pasteurization or sterilization with propylene oxide. Perhaps almonds are not the best example, because they can't be grown everywhere, but much produce can be. Does it make sense to grow lettuce thousands of miles away on huge, perhaps even organic, farms when it can be grown and tended locally by people who live nearby and are willing to work a few hours for a big box of produce every week? I certainly wouldn't mind picking almonds for a few hours during harvest season.

Again, what I am principally interested in is the connection between city dwellers and rural farms as the only fundamental way to instill aesthetic appreciation for the land.

I can understand objections that insist we can only feed the world's population with industrial agriculture. Handfuls of city people owning or working on local farms are not going to meet current, let alone future, demands. Agriculture must be big, specialized, monoculture to provide for the entire globe. So, at one level I agree it is silly to be looking at medieval models when we have a substantially larger population to feed on the same amount of land.

On the other hand, we will eventually reach (in fact, are rapidly approaching) a point in time when the majority of people not only know nothing about where their food comes from, but won't care anymore, and will stop subsidizing farms with tax dollars. Farming will simply cease to be profitable—as it already has in many places. Eventually, it may be outsourced like many other jobs. I believe the only way to reverse this trend is to get more people directly involved in some way, with financial or material incentives, sparking exactly the kind of appreciation for agriculture and food processing that we saw in Cato, Crescenzi, and Tanara.

Or we could even go one step further and follow Sir Thomas More. In his *Utopia* (1516), each city is surrounded by manors, where all citizens take turns living for two years at a time to work the farm. Each manor holds forty men and women and each year twenty are rotated off; the newcomers are trained by those who have been there a year. If a nation can arrange compulsory military service, why not compulsory agricultural service? In Utopia, the children are trained in agriculture at school, and regularly taken to the countryside, so everyone is skilled by the time they get there. More is explicit about why this is done: so everyone knows where food comes from, so everyone appreciates the labor that goes into producing food and values it, and so everyone knows what good food is.[13]

You might argue that today some people certainly know how to buy food that tastes good and is good for us, but something has gone terribly wrong when the majority of food is sold highly processed and prepackaged, miles away from where it was grown, often bearing little resemblance to what the farm produced. That will be the topic of the next chapter, but for the moment consider what Cato, Crescenzi, and Tanara plainly understood: knowing firsthand how food is cultivated and processed makes you appreciate it, makes you value quality over mere abundance and low cost. I think we should think less about maximizing yields at any cost—human and environmental—and start thinking about the aesthetic value of the farm and its importance to us not only for leisure, but for spiritual and economic nourishment. Only then will people be willing to pay more for food and think more conscientiously about everyone getting a fair share.

Cucina principale

lucerna

reditto da pavi

Camerino per garzoni

indegno

murello p pignatte

banco

Colonna col mortaro

Tauola per imbandire.

Cook Food

The past two decades have witnessed a meteoric rise of interest in food and cooking in the popular media. This has been manifest in bestselling cookbooks, an ever-growing number of cooking shows on multiple television networks, and brisk sales of food magazines (despite the demise of *Gourmet*). This interest has spilled over into academia. Food has become a serious object of study across the disciplines and there are several major encyclopedias, food book series, journals, conferences, and classes throughout college curricula.

Ironically, at the same time, there has been a decrease in actual home cooking. Home-cooked meals prepared from scratch declined from 72 percent of all meals eaten in 1980 to 59 percent in 2010.[1] With the exception of a few ardent souls who truly enjoy spending time in the kitchen, the majority of Americans consider cooking an odious chore, something to be finished as quickly and efficiently as possible so they can get back to doing other, more important, things. Thus people are perfectly satisfied with having others cook for them. Drive through the center of any city or suburb and you will find not only fast food chains, but the same half-dozen or so casual dining franchises, where the food is made in a factory, arrives frozen, and is microwaved to order. The proliferation is actually staggering; my son and I recently counted nineteen separate Subway sandwich shops where we live, in Stockton, California, a city of about 300,000. Most of the units are located within a radius of just a couple of miles, in the north part of the city.

When not eating out, those who don't cook are happy buying convenience foods—prepared meals frozen, canned, freeze-dried, or processed to such an extent that little action is required beyond heating. Stroll down the center aisles of any supermarket to witness the proliferation of ready-made and convenience foods. Processed food (as opposed to whole ingredients that must be cooked) accounts for 80 percent of food sold in the United States, in terms of profit. The USDA says we eat 31 percent more packaged food than fresh food, in terms of volume.[2]

Consumers trust the manufacturers of convenience food and are assured that what comes in the package will please their senses—and science guarantees that it will, not only with ample salt and sugar, but also with chemical flavors and fragrances that approximate the taste and aroma of real food. Consumers also trust that such prepared meals will sustain their bodies physiologically, socially, and perhaps even spiritually. By convenience food I mean anything ready to eat, or that only needs heating, so this includes much of the so-called health food, organic food, and nutraceutical fare among the fastest growing sectors of the food industry. Not only the latest açai berry bar and live lactobacillus acidophilus probiotic concoctions, but also organic Cheetos®. Add to that the many weight-loss programs that require purchasing frozen meals. Convenience foods are slowly insinuating themselves into every corner of the grocery: little plastic packages of cut-up apples (because children are apparently no longer aware of how to use their teeth) sprayed with chemicals, an entire aisle of breakfast cereals, another of crackers and cookies and snacks. But more notably, there are "complete," ready-made meals showing up everywhere. In the ethnic foods aisle there are boxes of pad thai, Mexican taco kits, vindaloo in a bag—pretty much anything to prevent you from actually trying to cook these foods. Even the butcher pre-marinates, pre-stuffs, and precooks the pre-cut-up meat that is now processed elsewhere. Don't forget those things that give the illusion of cooking—cake mixes, cookie dough or biscuits in a tube, prebaked pizza dough. All these ultimately lure the consumer away from cooking foods from scratch, even though it is usually much less expensive and just as easy to do so.

Whether this was a kind of conspiracy on the part of the food industry to enslave the public is immaterial; the results are incontrovertible. To maximize profit margins (Tater Tots® cost much more than the same weight of potatoes), the proliferation of convenience foods has left nearly an entire hapless generation bereft of many of the most basic cooking skill sets. We have become de-skilled. Many cooking techniques have become almost entirely obsolete because they require time and patience. A 2010 Department of Labor survey says that the average American (as household head) spent thirty-two minutes each day preparing food and cleaning up.[3] That is compared to two hours and forty-five minutes watching TV. It also seems ironic that the more obsessed Americans become with watching cooking on TV, the less they actually do it. A similar situation, one might argue, applies to sports and sex. Even more ironically, eating, moving our bodies physically, and reproducing are three of our species's most essential biological functions. We would not survive without these behaviors, and yet, we let professionals do it while we watch. Perhaps it is the perception that professionals do these so well that discourages us from even trying. In any case, the more we watch others cook, the less we do it ourselves, and perversely, the less we know how to do it.

But if we have become de-skilled, then our ancestors must have been proficient in the kitchen; if not our parents' generation then maybe our grandparents' a century or more ago. The historian in me must ask, what kind of evidence can prove that? While numerous studies have shown our own lack of confidence in the kitchen in recent years, no studies exist showing that in the past, people routinely executed complicated culinary tasks. The fact that such procedures are amply described in cookbooks is certainly no evidence; perhaps just as today, people were armchair chefs, merely fantasizing about cooking grand recipes and throwing magnificent dinner parties. That is, cookbooks are never a good record of what people actually ate. They are more often aspirational; prescriptive rather than descriptive. Moreover, although we tend to think that the proliferation of fast food and casual dining spots is a modern phenomenon, there have always been, at least in cities, quick, inexpensive places to eat out, such as taverns, saloons, lunch counters, and cafeterias. It may come as a surprise that many apartments in the nineteenth century did not include cooking facilities, and many people lived in boarding houses where meals were provided. On the other hand, until the twentieth century, a much greater percentage of people lived outside cities, and someone, most likely the farmer's wife, did the cooking. Not that this cooking was necessarily complex, but it was cooking—transforming raw ingredients into palatable nourishment.

We do know that with the rise of industrial food processing in the late nineteenth century, many basic procedures became obsolete in home cooking. Many factors were involved, including transportation, refrigeration technology, increasing urbanization, and marketing and branding. All these were bound to make consumers less knowledgeable about the origins of ingredients and how to deal with such foodstuffs. Slaughtering animals could only legally be done by professionals with inspectors present, thanks to stringent health regulations—necessary when the scale and speed of slaughter made careful monitoring more difficult. While rural families might still have practiced home canning, most people purchased foods in tin cans, which was preferred for its scientific cleanliness, consistency, and reliability. Instead of curing meat at home, people relied on Armour®, Swift, or Oscar Mayer. When it came to cheese, local dairies gave way to Kraft, who could afford the new pasteurization equipment. All these procedures were deemed simply not possible to do at home. In the interest of scientifically controlled safety standards, factories took over these household tasks, manufacturing standardized, homogenous, and, one could argue, aesthetically inferior products. But they were considered safe and hygienic. No doubt there were accidental poisonings in the past. A whole family might get sick from eating something spoiled, though wide-scale outbreaks of *E. coli, listeria*, and other pathogens were simply not possible because food was not processed on the same scale or shipped as far. Without contemporary surveys, we have little knowledge of the scale of such activities before industrialization, but it is undeniable that the expertise in how to make such foods has progressively diminished, especially as agriculture itself was mechanized and fewer people lived on farms, as women entered the workplace in greater numbers, and as messy physical labor in the kitchen was increasingly seen as demeaning.[4]

We lost not only these preservation techniques, but fundamental cooking skills, such as making stock from scratch rather than using a bouillon cube or can, shelling fresh peas rather than opening a frozen bag of Bird's Eye®, or even baking fresh bread using locally milled flour and wild starters. All these took time, and since time was to be spent either in productive, money-making work, or in leisurely escape, time spent in the kitchen when you could be elsewhere was simply time wasted.

This line of reasoning, I will argue, has left us profoundly disconnected from our food in ways that are dangerous socially, environmentally, culturally, and indeed aesthetically if we consider the quality of much industrial food. Now we have seen the rise of many artisanal products, excellent cheese, bread, local jams and such, and these are superb. But they are still by and large things we leave to others to make, and they are products that for the most part are expensive luxuries, not everyday items or household staples. They are not things most people routinely create.

So what I will propose is looking to the past, relearning those techniques which were once described in cookbooks, which practically no one does anymore, and which have almost completely vanished from the culinary literature. The question I hope will arise immediately is, Why? Why do something difficult and perhaps even dangerous, when you can let someone else do it? I contend that making your own food is not only inherently entertaining, but connects you to food in a direct and palpable way, such that it makes you a more social, responsible, and spiritually fulfilled individual.

Equally important to the rise of industrial food has been a distressing evolution of the culinary literature itself in the past century. For example, think of the modern recipe format: a list of ingredients, precise measurements and cooking times, and detailed instructions suggesting that even the slightest alteration will lead you down the path of complete disaster. Following a recipe with such pseudo-scientific precision is simply not necessary for the majority of dishes. I understand completely why modern cookbook authors write this way. They want to copyright their work, they want their work to be unique and new in order to sell cookbooks, and the tendency is to dumb down directions to sell more; remove messy and difficult recipes so the cooking seems quick and easy. But in requiring strict adherence to seemingly scientific recipes, they are actually complicit in this process of de-skilling. It is comparable to following directions from a GPS device, which tells you exactly where and when to turn, so you never learn to navigate intuitively. People are led to turn onto railroad tracks or into a river, in the same way I've heard of food left burning in the oven because it hasn't cooked for the prescribed length of time, or recipes not being prepared because one small ingredient was missing.

I think to better serve the public, cookbooks should instruct people how to cook, teaching techniques and procedures rather than precise recipes. They should explain ingredients, rather than ways to cut corners. They should be more like cookbooks written a hundred or several hundred years ago, offering an approach to the endeavor, not just strict formulas. This will ultimately make us not only more proficient in the kitchen, but more conscientious about what we eat, more responsible consumers who pay attention to the environment, animal welfare, food security, and the real cost of food. I think it all starts with actually cooking food, eating it only at its seasonal peak, not wasting parts because we're squeamish, and most importantly, not buying anything simply because we think it will save time and be convenient.

I have to admit that my initial approach to old cookbooks was as a food historian. That is, I was interested primarily in what cookbooks reveal about the past, by way of the available ingredients and cooking technologies mentioned. I considered potential readership, the social setting of food preparation, and who was actually in the kitchen. Cookbooks have a lot to say about the social meaning of food, the kinds of values and aspirations cookbook authors espoused either in domestic or professional settings, and what the daily experience of cooks might have entailed. Typically, such analysis offers concrete details about class, gender, sometimes ethnicity or nationality, but it misses in a very fundamental way the aesthetic basis of historic culinary practices. What did food taste like in the past?

So I began to actually cook old recipes, using antiquated tools and fuel sources, following recipes without cutting corners or adapting them in any way. I was convinced that if one were to veer even an inch from the historic recipe, one would ultimately learn nothing about the past at all. And there were a number of important discoveries I made about early modern techniques, including how to roast using a turnspit beside an open flame, how to braise in clay vessels over hot coals, and how sauces were once combined with a wide range of spices, pounded in a mortar, thickened with breadcrumbs, moistened with verjuice, and sieved. These recipes actually only make sense when you physically do them and taste them.

If the ultimate purpose here is to learn something about the past, then I still contend that one must stick as close as possible to the original recipes. Even when their directions are imprecise, a little context and practice means you can closely follow them without "faking it." But there does come a certain point when one realizes that certain conditions simply cannot be replicated. The soil produces different fruits and vegetables than in the past, the climate and weather conditions are not the same, the animals have been bred for particular characteristics (for example, in the case of pork, the flesh is much leaner than in the past). So while the culinary historian must stick to the recipe, the practical home cook reviving bygone techniques must learn through experience how available ingredients work, and how the local yeasts and bacteria behave from season to season. Ultimately, the old cookbooks do teach techniques but they cannot be followed scrupulously or archaeologically. And it is my contention that most old cookbooks were never meant to be used that way. They were designed to teach people how to cook.

This may seem paradoxical, but to learn from cookbooks of the past, we must actually abandon their directions when local ingredients, conditions, and bacteria so dictate. The knowledge that is gained from an intimate connection to one's ingredients and tools, to the changes of season, to differences in temperature, ultimately frees the cook from the recipe. Furthermore, it is only when you begin to really work with local conditions that you come to understand how best to deal with ingredients and processes— and that means abandoning cookbooks, both old and new. Only then do you come to realize how fulfilling these processes can be, how they can be incorporated into the rhythms of daily life, and how, though seemingly time consuming, this kind of work is actually much more rewarding than letting someone else prepare food for you. It is certainly more economical, and the food almost always tastes better.

I would like to recount the basic outlines of three fermentation projects that began as experiments and eventually became completely routine—they concern bread, salami, and cheese. If you pick up one of the many baking cookbooks available today, you will find meticulously exacting recipes, some requiring weighing the flour, feeding a starter three times a day, or specialized convection ovens. I don't know who has patience for this, although I'm sure one could make excellent bread following their directions.[5] But I doubt they would ever successfully veer from the directions. I'm not sure the bread ever really becomes theirs, so to speak, or that they really learn how to bake intuitively. Moreover, using commercial yeast, you get a very dependable but pretty boring bread, mostly because the yeast is too strong. It's bred for speed, but doesn't require the time necessary to allow the flavor to really develop.

With this in mind, you can turn to history. There aren't many cookbooks explicit about baking bread, but some, such as Gervase Markham's seventeenth-century *The English Housewife*, offers a few clues.[6] First is the making of a starter. Markham describes manchet made with ale barm, but also a sour leaven that is broken up in warm water and then strained. But he doesn't mention how to make the leaven in the first place. It turns out sourdough starters need not be saved for years. They can be easily made in about two weeks. Just leave a bowl of flour and water out on the counter, feed it with a little more flour and water every morning and eventually it will bubble, smell sour, and be strong enough to use. Markham is then probably saving some of the dough from each batch to make a kind of starter batter, but another way to do it is to just use a cup or two of the starter directly in making each new dough. If you bake a big batch of bread every week, the pot of starter should never overflow. The dough is merely a few cups of starter, a cup of water, about a tablespoon of salt, and enough flour to make a firm dough, nothing more. It is kneaded for about ten minutes, left to rise, knocked down and kneaded again, and left to rise for between four and twelve hours, entirely dependent on the weather and the whim of the starter.

There are a few other tricks, such as keeping a baking stone in the oven, sprinkling water inside the hot oven to create steam, and especially slashing the bread before it goes into the oven to allow it to lift upwards. A wicker brotform basket for the dough to rise in is also nice and creates beautiful ridged spirals. This technique made not only artisan-quality bread, but bread made with my own local yeast and lactobacillus. It was, so to speak, *my* bread.

But it also occurred to me that industrially milled bread flour can be grown anywhere, milled somewhere else, and shipped across the country. An antiquated milling technique would probably yield very different results. Remarkably, a stone quern is something that can be purchased online. It is simply two large millstones, cut with ridges on the interior, which break and grind the wheat berries. The technology is paleolithic. You pour whole wheat into a hole in the top, turn the handle, and the wheat sprinkles out from the edge where the two stones meet. It then needs to be sifted to remove the coarser bran, and can even be finely bolted through cloths to make white flour. Freshly milled wheat behaves differently from regular flour. It absorbs water more slowly, is more difficult to knead, and makes a considerably denser bread. It is excellent, nonetheless.

But I still didn't get a sense that it had anything to do with the place. For that, one would need locally grown wheat. In the nineteenth century, it was actually the most important crop where I live, in Stockton, which is why the Caterpillar tractor was invented right here by Benjamin Holt—to prevent the wheels of the harvesters from sinking into the muddy soil. They were replaced with a circular metal tread, like you see on a tank. Wheat is still grown in the area to some extent, though not easy to find, and certainly not sold in small packages. After many harrowing phone calls to various agencies, the Wheat Board of California was nice enough to send me a five-pound bag.

An opportunity to go one step further presented itself one summer when I was touring an experimental farm in Finland with a group of ethnographers. No one seemed to mind that I pocketed a few samples of wheat and rye. It was maybe a handful or less. I smuggled them home, sprouted them in a ziplock bag on the window sill, and planted them in a big clay pot. They grew tall, and in the spring I mowed them with a sharp machete, beat the sheaf with a makeshift flail, and winnowed the grains in a basket (essentially, you just toss them up and let the wind blow away the chaff). After this whole procedure, my yield was a little bit more than a handful of grain—enough for a small bun. But I did make a new starter from the grains, so at least some of them and their bacteria went into bread.

The final step naturally involved building a bread oven. I was determined not to spend a fortune following plans for a professional oven using refractory bricks. People in the past used clay and straw and built them by hand. I wanted something a little more permanent, that could remain uncovered year-round. I think in retrospect I would have formed the oven and fired it in place, but since I have a kiln in my basement pottery studio, I thought making my own bricks would be fun. In brief, the oven was made on a raised platform of cinderblocks. There was a base of clay about four inches thick, covered with a hemispherical mound of wet sand, on top of which another four-inch layer of clay was placed. I cut holes for the chimney and door, and then cut the entire oven into bricks, labeling each one with a letter and number so I could replace them in exactly the same order (which proved more difficult than I imagined). The bricks were dried for a few weeks and fired in three separate batches to earthenware temperature, or about 1,800 degrees. I then reassembled them with mortar, filling up the interior again with sand to support the curvature of the brick courses. I have a newly acquired respect for bricklaying; it is a lot more difficult than it looks, especially with weirdly shaped bricks. After drying, a thick layer of stucco was applied as insulation, and the sand was removed from the interior.

I have to admit, learning how to fire such a beast takes a lot of patience. My first batches of bread and pizza came out with sand in the crust. Hint: vacuum out the interior! The right amount and type of fuel to use was tricky. Sometimes the oven was too hot and the bread crust charred immediately before the insides had a chance to cook. It turns out my oven prefers small, relatively thin sticks rather than logs, and with an hour's stoking, she stays hot for several hours, enough to bake bread and then put in a casserole or joint of meat to roast. I am still learning the subtle nuances of how to cook in the oven, but it is perfectly mesmerizing to watch while it heats up, especially at night. The idea that I am cooking the same way people did hundreds of years ago is among the most thrilling things on earth to me.

Ultimately, however, you are likely wondering, What is the point? Apart from historical research, this is clearly an entirely impractical way to make bread. In my regular weekly baking routine, I admit, I use the conventional oven. But the experiment made me intimately knowledgeable about what makes good bread—something I could never have learned from a book or even from watching someone else do it. I think the more people take the time to cook from scratch, even if not using such traditional methods as these, they would come to appreciate food much more. They would also reject the mass-produced travesties that pass for bread in the grocery stores. There is of course some very good bread out there. But I think the quality would rise immeasurably; we would see a resurgence of village bakers serving bread that reflects local preferences and *terroir* (the taste of the place—a combination of soil, climate, situation, and human skill), and good bread would become much more widely available locally, rather than the faux rustic bread found at supermarkets. Most importantly, more people would be inspired to bake bread themselves.

Let me share a technique on making salami and how it was reconstructed. Very little has been recorded in food literature about this. Cookbooks, for example, often tell you how to serve cured meats, and very often give directions for various cooked sausages, but the actual curing was always done either by professionals in cities or on a small scale on farms where the pigs were slaughtered. Bartolomeo Scappi, writing in 1570, for example, describes the products, but says it isn't his profession, and stops there.[7] *Salumi* (all cured pork products) wasn't something chefs regularly made. But there are glimpses here and there.

In Christoforo di Messisbugo's *Banchetti*, from 1549, there is a recipe that reads:

> Take two pounds of pork meat and a pound of beef, and pound everything well together, and for each pound of meat add half an ounce of salt and 6 grains of crushed pepper, a little fennel according to your judgment, and mix everything well then "invest" this stuff, well pressed down into a washed pig's bung *"e cura te, come le altre sopradette"* ["and cure it like the ones above"].[8]

The "above ones" he either lets dry on their own, or in smoke. The recipe is simple, if terse, but there is really nothing more to it. Not to accidentally poison myself, I decided to read up on everything that could be found about curing meats, and even interviewed one of the leading manufacturers of traditional salami in the United States, Paul Bertolli. What I learned is that due to federal regulations no one actually makes salami with traditional curing methods. They always use bacterial starters, which lower the pH quickly, and to my taste, make the meat overly sour and slightly slimy. They also use potassium nitrite (rather than traditional saltpeter), which I surmised was not a bad idea since a cold anaerobic atmosphere is ideal for the growth of botulism.

With these dangers in mind, I decided to add nitrates. I am pretty sure they were naturally present in mined salt in the past (*sal petrae* merely means rock salt). Today, commercial refining of salt always purifies it into sodium chloride, with everything else removed. Sea salt is less refined but doesn't contain enough nitrates to cure meat effectively. So for long-cured salami I use Instacure #2 (sodium nitrite and sodium nitrate), or sometimes celery juice powder, which is actually less dependable. When you see on a package of bacon, hot dogs, or ham that it's "uncured," that's just a lie. The celery powder contains nitrates naturally, but legally it can only be sold as organic if it doesn't contain mined nitrates. Someday I hope to make saltpeter, which involves a large pile of rotting bird manure. Whatever the source, it is essentially the same chemical. It is necessary not only for long storage but to bring out the rosy red color of salami and ham. I think it lends cured products a particularly appealing flavor and texture as well.[9]

There is nothing complicated about the procedure. You don't need any machines at all, just salt, Instacure, intestines, and a sharp knife. As long as the fat-to-meat ratio is about 25 percent to 75 percent, you just chop the meat finely and stuff it into the casings—with a funnel in the case of the narrow pig's intestines, or by hand with beef middles or the very large "bung," which is what is normally used for *mortadella* and *salame toscano*. The bung is the cul de sac, or fermentation chamber, in a cow, which has only one opening and holds about ten pounds of meat or more. You simply tie the casings up with twine and put them somewhere that stays about 55 degrees Fahrenheit with high humidity. A cave would be perfect, but I used my wine fridge, which maintains a constant temperature of about 55 degrees. You can also introduce white mold into the cave by putting in an already cured *salame*.

I have been making salami this way for several years now, and have never seen one spoil as long as it remained in the "cave." Moreover, it is completely different from the way commercial salami is made in the United States. The discovery in this case is that the technique, when not tampered with using modern equipment or chemical additives, allows the natural bacteria thriving where I live in California to cure the meat in a way that reflects our local *terroir*. There would be no way to replicate exactly the cured meat of Italy from 500 years ago, nor the bread nor cheese for that matter, but by following the traditional curing methods, one can make an excellent product that reflects the local biota of any particular location, which is exactly how, out of necessity, people in the past would have done it.

The lesson learned, once again, is that by using technologies of the past, whether followed to the letter from cookbooks, or letting ambient bacteria and molds do the work exactly as they did in the past, one can get a much more accurate estimation of bygone culinary aesthetics. Best of all, I started making salami on a regular basis, keeping the cellar stocked and starting another batch every few weeks. Like the bread, it fit into my regular kitchen rhythms, and a five-pound batch, after curing, lasts about a month in my household. It doesn't take a great deal of time, maybe an hour every month or so.

Like the bread and cured meat, cheese is something you can learn to do through modern cookbooks. There are dozens of guides. Some things you have to buy, like rennet, which otherwise requires access to a calf's stomach. Suppliers will also furnish forms, presses, bacterial starters, and various chemicals and mold, to give you exactly the kinds of cheese you want regardless of where you live. Their protocols work well, but you have to follow procedures meticulously.

But what if you depended solely on natural bacteria, molds, and fungi that are everywhere and have traditionally been the only way to make cheese? Since the discovery of bacteria over a century ago, food manufacturers have removed as many of the unpredictable microbes as they could and replaced them with standardized strains. This has happened to wine and beer, bread yeast, pickles, cheese, and *salumi*—all fermented products. Of course in the process, much of the uniqueness of particular places has been lost. The food is, admittedly, safer, more consistent, and travels better, but it often pales in comparison to naturally made products. In the case of cheese, more than any other food, pasteurization has almost completely killed the wonderful variety of local flavors. Or at least it has been consistently heading in that direction until recently.

Like bread and salami, cheese mostly makes itself. So the story goes, our neolithic ancestor was transporting milk in a stomach bag container strapped to the side of his horse, and after a long, jiggling ride, discovered that the contents of his bag had coagulated into curds and whey. But you don't even need a stomach bag for that outcome. Bacteria will naturally sour and separate milk. This seems odd to modern people who know that milk goes bad after a week. Actually, that only happens when milk is pasteurized, when it's been heated to kill all the bacteria, good and bad, along with most of the flavor. Pasteurized milk does indeed rot if kept too long—even with refrigeration. But raw milk turns sour and tangy when invaded by lactobacilli. They lower the pH and kill off other bad bacteria. With the right bacteria, the milk will solidify into something like yoghurt, and can then be drained and stored as a kind of cheese. This is a natural process that any neolithic herdsman would have known well. The major technological advance was understanding how rennet sets the milk much quicker, allowing the curds to be drained off the whey after a few hours.

If you are also wondering who in their right mind would have thought to add an enzyme found in a calf's stomach (rennet) to milk, consider that in order to keep cows producing milk, they have to become pregnant, and half of their offspring will naturally be male veal calves, unprofitable except as meat. And it would also have been apparent in slaughter that the stomach contents of the calf consisted of curdled milk—the first stage of cheese. In other words, cheese was more or less discovered, it didn't need to be invented.

The advantage of cheese over milk is that it can be stored and more easily transported. If we want to get a sense of the early methods of preservation, useful especially in hot climates, I think the best example of what an early cheese would have been like is *feta*. It's a young, fresh cheese, not aged, but preserved in brine. In this case, the salt prevents spoilage and the water prevents excessive drying. In fine curd cheeses like *chèvre*, they are wrapped in leaves or ashes to prevent drying, but ultimately, unless eaten, they become rock hard and only good for grating.

Younger and fresher cheeses with large curds, like cottage cheese, require salt and need to be pressed to remove excess moisture, which would cause spoilage. In ancient times this was done in a simple willow basket or forma (hence the Italian word *formaggio*), sometimes with a weight on top. Thereafter, the rind is encouraged, in some cheeses by washing the rind and letting mold develop. The rind prevents the interior from drying out and allows the cheese to age, becoming sharper, sometimes allowing the molecular structure of the proteins to change—as in *Parmigiano*, with that crunchy, crystalline bite. Other cheeses, like cheddar, are wrapped in bandages, or covered in wax like Gouda. The point of a rind is to create a barrier, which at first lets moisture out but then with the help of natural molds prevents other microbes from getting in. (The mold on salami works exactly the same way, as a kind of gate keeper—and in both cases, molds add flavor.)

There are many descriptions of cheese making going back to ancient times, even an entire book on it in the fifteenth century by Pantaleone da Confienza. There's also a detailed description of how to make Swiss cheese in the sixteenth century by Jacob Bifrons.[10]

I must also mention a remarkable little book written in praise of *Piacentino* cheese called *Formaggiata di Sere Stentato* written by Giulio Landi.[11] *Formaggiata* sort of means to become "becheesed" and the book is a burlesque, with many risqué references and double entendres in praise of sausages or melons. It often reads like ad copy and even concludes with an argument over trade descriptions, asserting that *Piacentino* shouldn't be confused with or labeled as *Parmigiano* or *Milanese*. It sounds remarkably modern to me, even if it gets silly at times.

The book's author is described in the preface as a courteous gentleman who delights in the aroma of ravioli, is pleased by a good mouthful, and is especially fond of the cheese from his own city. For him, the quality of the cheese is a matter of *terroir* (*la natura de i terreni*), the herbs on which the cows feed, the fresh air and water. Naturally the cows here are fatter, healthier, and stronger than those from other places. He continues that, of course, the most noble beasts in Italy produce the best cheese, but it also has to do with the salt there, which is finer and whiter than sea salt and lends excellent flavor to the food, especially the salami, which is the best in Italy, plus *cervelate, mortadella, sanguinacci,* and *zambudelli* (various types of sausage). The salt must have a kind of secret occult quality, and he insists that the locals don't need doctors. He then argues that the perfection of the circular form, not to mention the size, make *Piacentino* the king of cheeses. Landi doesn't tell us how to make cheese, but it is worth noting that he recognizes the importance of place and distinctive ingredients. In other words, where you make the cheese is just as important as how—an important lesson.

There are many other fascinating cheese history sources from this period. For example, Agostino Gallo, in *Le vinti giornata di agricultura*,[12] offers fairly detailed directions for making cheese, as he knew it in his native Brescia—which is on the road between Milan and Verona, right at the foot of the Alps. He explains how after coagulation, the *giuncata* (coagulated milk) is heated on a gentle fire and broken up with a stick. Then the cheese maker plunges his bare (and clean) arms to the bottom of the pot and stirs gently to make sure all the curds are equally cooked. He then carefully lifts the curds out and places them on a white cloth or in a basin. A wooden board is placed on top and weights added so the superfluous "broth" seeps out. Then the cheese is dried, salted, etc. I found particularly interesting his comment that the length of time one heats the curds will determine how much salt it will absorb, as does the season. I think he's very perceptive that a few degrees difference in temperature and even an extra few minutes over the fire really does have a dramatic effect on the final product. It's also very clear that he has experimented with various procedures. For example, he says many people, after removing the exterior salt, will rub the cheese with olive oil, but he insists that linseed oil is better. Gallo even reveals his mistakes—he says if after aging you find cracks, there's really no remedy. Eat the cheese yourself or try to sell it for whatever you can.

But it's not until the last few hundred years that such descriptions have been detailed enough to really learn from. Tanara's cheese instructions mentioned in the last chapter are quite good, but for the details of the procedure, eighteenth-century cheese expert Josiah Twamley, in his book *Dairying Exemplified*, was absolutely indispensable.[13] Most importantly, he doesn't offer precise instructions, he basically just describes the process, tells you everything that can go right or wrong and actually teaches you how to make cheese. Keep in mind, using his text requires intentionally not paying any attention to modern cheese-making techniques.

Let me give you a very brief overview of how it is done. First, you must start with raw milk. Nothing would have been pasteurized in his day. I used a fairly local cow's milk, which is legal to sell in California. It must be about 90 degrees, cow temperature, and kept there long enough for ambient bacteria to thrive. In the process of heating it, be sure the milk is not too hot or, as Twamley says, you will have "sweet, or funkey cheese." Next, you mix twenty drops of liquid rennet into cold water, blend it with the milk, and leave it alone. After about an hour or so, it doesn't curdle but solidifies into a gelatinous mass. This is cut with a knife and left to exude whey. Twamley doesn't use the word, but the process today is called "cheddaring." This sits another half-hour or so, still at 90 degrees. Then the heat is turned up to about 98 degrees. More whey exudes, and you see long strips of cheese start to come together and sink to the bottom. It will be ready when the whey is no longer white but "you will always find the whey quite green" says Twamley. In fall, the whey takes on a bluish hue.

After that, it is a simple matter of pouring off the whey little by little, salting the curds lightly, and putting them into a cheesecloth-lined strainer to drip further. At this point, you can make the cheese into mozzarella, let it set as a simple white cheese, or press it. Pressing can be done simply with a large weight placed on top, and something for the whey to drip into. I sometimes use a spaghetti pot with strainer insert. The cheese is left to dry for a few days, then is wrapped in cloth smeared with lard, and left in the cave for about six months. The smaller the cheese, the quicker it dries out; I've found at home that two gallons is about the upper limit, which makes a nice-sized truckle of superb white cheddar—piquant, with little crunchy crystals, not unlike *Parmigiano* in some respects. From the remaining whey, you can make *ricotta* or Norwegian *mysost*—simply by cooking down the whey for hours until it caramelizes like fudge. In America, this is sold as *gjetost*, definitely worth trying if you don't make it yourself.

Now the real reason to do all these things is not primarily health (though people are making grand claims for live bacteria these days), it is not chiefly cost (though preparing foods yourself from scratch definitely can be cheaper), it's not even taste. There are professionals who can do these things better than you. The reason to do it is primarily for the fun. Plus there is the connection it gives you to other living beings—those you eat, and those with whom you share the food. That's the subject of my last chapter.

CONCORDIA

Melius est vocari ad olera cum charitate   En pape auons contentement   Besser ein weinig ist mit lieb
Quam ad Vitulum saginatum cum odio.   En Noises tout desbauchement   Dan viel auß haß vnd mit betrub

PAX ALIT INGENIA, ET PRÆCLARAS EXCITAT ARTES, PAX HOMINI LARGA DAT BONA CVNCTA MANV.

Share Food

When my wife and I decided to have a family, I said I would let her make all the rules as long as I was allowed to make one that could never be broken: that we would always eat together as a family. When my children got older, if someone didn't want to eat what I was cooking, and admittedly it was sometimes strange, that was fine. I was happy to cook whatever anyone wanted, as long as we sat down at the table together and ate. Sometimes I regret offering choices, especially when I end up cooking several different meals in one night, and then having to eat the same leftovers several days thereafter. And I will admit, sometimes the rule does get broken nowadays, when someone has a play rehearsal or some other activity going on in the evening. Sometimes one of the adults is away for work, usually me. But the rule still stands. I also have to admit that it isn't always pleasant. My two sons fight all the time, and the table is often the place where all the frustrations and anxieties of the day are gathered and then taken out on everyone else.

The reason for this rule is really not a fundamental belief that family meals somehow make families stick together, which in turn makes communities cohere, which instills values in children, lowers crime rates, and maintains the order of society. There is a lot of ideological baggage associated with family meals, or the supposed breakdown of them. Some people see the demise of the family meal as the cause of the erosion of the traditional family itself, and as the root of all of society's evils. Sometimes they go so far as to blame women who work outside the home—if only those wives and mothers would get back into the kitchen and cook for their families, everything would be right again.

I don't agree with this simple equation. Pathologically criminal people who eat with their children are going to mess them up. I don't think a family meal magically makes everything better or upholds traditional families. Nor would historians agree that there ever was such a thing as a "traditional family," meaning two heterosexual parents with two and a half children (I always felt bad for that half a kid). Single parent households, extended households including relatives—a whole variety of different forms have been common through history, sometimes very effective at instilling positive values across generations, but not always.

Nonetheless, I am going to argue for the importance not only of eating together as a family, but the importance of sharing meals communally, with neighbors, colleagues, fellow citizens. I will draw examples of food rituals from history, and offer a kind of typology of how sharing food functions socially. First, I should point out that my original motives for making a family dinner rule in my household were purely selfish. I grew up mostly eating alone in front of the TV. That was never an intentional plan, but in suburbia, the commute for my dad into the city became more and more congested and stretched from an hour to more than two, so by the time he got home it was very late. It made sense to feed me earlier. My siblings are much older and left for college when I was still quite young. So, it was usually just me for dinner, plus Gilligan and the Skipper, Ginger and Mary Ann . . .

There is no doubt that eating with other people serves a social function within families and groups. Getting together with others is almost unthinkable without food being involved in some way. Sharing in and of itself, giving of one's labor for the sustenance of others, is inherently pleasurable. I always think the more work someone put in, the more they made the food their own, the greater it should be appreciated. If a cake is homemade, it means more than one that is purchased. Assuming there aren't mitigating circumstances that everyone deals with now and then, the store-bought version says, "I don't care enough about you to put time into preparing something good; I have more important things to do, so I'll just go out and buy any old junk, and you won't know the difference, because you have no taste anyway." French gastronome Brillat-Savarin put it best: "He who receives his friends and gives no personal attention to the meal which is being prepared for them, is not worthy of having friends."

Anthropologists and archaeologists have long speculated about the role of eating communally in human evolution, how hunting and gathering required cooperation and complex language skills, how cooking food drew people together in front of a fire, allowed them to share stories, perhaps even facilitated larger brain capacity, as less energy was spent just digesting food. Cooking may be the very reason we evolved in the first place, according to Richard Wrangham.[1] These gatherings around the fire certainly did teach values and helped the group cohere as a social unit, encouraging people to protect and care for each other.

Historians, on the other hand, dependent on the written word, can only go back a few thousand years before the common era. The earliest information we have about foodstuffs are recorded on cuneiform tablets, basically counting heads of cattle and bushels of grain, and of course assessing property—fixed and movable—for taxation purposes. Writing systems only exist when you have a state that needs to count material possessions so it can maintain itself through taxation, and that goes back to ancient Sumer. Hence, the earliest written texts are all about food. The Epic of Gilgamesh recounts how the wild man Enkidu is tamed so that he can be a human companion for the hero; he is seduced by a harlot, eats bread, and drinks a lot of beer. That's what it takes to make him human and civilized. The earliest texts are also about feasting and sacrifice.

Let's start with feasting. Historically, a meal eaten with other people is an expression of power and social relationships. When a chieftain gathers his warriors around and feeds them, when a Viking leader brings his thanes into the mead hall, or when a king invites the aristocracy into his palace for a formal banquet, each powerful figure is essentially reminding his guests of their subservience. A power lunch among office executives is fairly similar. In medieval banquets, the lord of the manor would sit physically higher than others, on a dais—the last remnant of which is a wedding party seated only on one side of a table, raised so everyone else can see guests of honor perform the meal. On the medieval dais, there would be a large, ornamental salt cellar, so everyone else would be literally "below the salt." Where you sat was also important—those closest to the host were the most honored guests, and strangely enough they would often be offered food from the head table, once the hosts were done with it. To be seated in the far corner was much like getting put in front of the bathroom door in a fashionable restaurant. It said, you are not important. The same thing happened at ancient Roman dinner parties. The satirist Juvenal complained of being invited to dinner and then being served stale, old, measly food while the host had fine wines, elegant exotic dishes, and expensive luxuries.[2] The message was intentional: Important people sit close to me and get similar food, the people I want to belittle are far away. Just think how odd that is to our modern sensibilities. It would be like getting invited to dinner and being served a McDonald's hamburger while the host was eating filet mignon. We like to think of ourselves as all equal (a fiction of course), so everyone gets the same food in the same proportion, but it's a way we uphold the pretense of equality. Most historical banquets were exactly the opposite. They were a staging of inequality. Although I'm certainly not suggesting we imitate this treatment of guests, at least the participants were being open and honest about their relationships.

The other common feature of ancient food texts, also something we have largely lost in most modern societies, is sacrifice. We tend to think in a very simple way that sacrifice is about giving up something because it will make you stronger, show God you are serious, or somehow make you more spiritual, because you are going without some physically pleasing luxury. But in the ancient texts, a sacrifice is about offering food to feed the gods or ancestral spirits. The Orishas in Yoruba worship even have their own particular favorite foods. In many traditions, the gods don't have bodies, so they can't physically consume the food, they just look down and appreciate it in an immaterial way, or they smell the smoke that rises from burning fat thrown on the sacrificial altar. This is how Yahweh, the God of the ancient Hebrews, enjoyed unspotted lambs; the fat and entrails or sometimes the whole animal was burned and "it is an odor pleasing unto the Lord."[3] (Mmm, barbecue.) Similarly, the *havan* of ancient Vedic times was a sacred fire on which ghee or animals were burnt as an offering to Vishnu or Shiva, as a way to literally convey food to the gods in a form they could use.

In most types of sacrifice, the food is simply placed on a table before an image of the god, as when monks make offerings to Buddha, or when a table is set out for the festival of San Giuseppe heaped with sweets, breads in the form of carpenter's tools, and fava beans. Similarly, in Day of the Dead celebrations in Mexico, favorite foods of departed ancestors are arranged on a special table. Most ancient cultures had some form of sacrifice that entailed the partial destruction of foods, and often the consumption of the rest by the priests or by the community.

The question is, Why would people, perhaps on the threshold of starvation, make a sacrifice and destroy something they could otherwise eat? The first thing Noah does when he gets off the ark is make a sacrifice—after saving all those animals, he kills one. The rationale is usually not merely feeding the gods; it is also about the ritual itself, an act of public, prescribed appeasement. Note that the food set aside must be the best, and it must be given first to a ritually pure intermediary, a priest of some kind who performs the sacrifice. And the gods don't always accept it; the sacrifice can be refused, much as a prayer or any act of supplication. It's not an automatic exchange, or else we would be compelling the gods to act a certain way, and that would be power we have over them.

The point is that people are trying to gain God's favor. They are giving him what he really wants, which is obedience, fear, dependency, and only incidentally food. Significantly, it is done every year at the same time, in a sacred space, and is always done in the same way, with the same formulaic words chanted to make the offering. It is really about the ritual itself. The fact that food is being offered can also be a kind of Thanksgiving. The original meaning of the term (rather than the specific American holiday) is a ritual of acknowledging benefits bestowed, such as a bountiful harvest. The benefit could also be averting some disaster, which is traditionally why St. Joseph is honored—for sparing a town in Sicily from a famine, by sending rain. So this is not merely a feast or an opportunity to eat a lot, it is food set aside as an offering, as an expression of thanks or to ask for a good blessing or particular favor.

But let me return to the destruction of the animal or foodstuff. A sacrifice today is just prepared food set out, but in the past it involved ritual slaughter. People watching were meant to see the blood flung around the altar, or the human heart still pumping raised up to Huitzlipochtli, or the chicken with its throat slit swung over the priest's head in Santeria. It was meant to be terrifying. The reason, I think, is because blood is a scary substance. Just the sight of it makes many people swoon. It is matter out of place, and numinous—we tremble in its presence, but are also drawn to it with fascination. We can easily imagine it coursing through our own veins and when it is spilled (as it must be in kosher ritual: the blood is the life and it belongs to God), we get a vivid sense of our own mortality. We empathize with the victim. That is hardwired into us biologically: the rush of adrenaline, the quickening heart rate, the inability to turn away.

It's also important to note that the sacrifice is not merely asking for favors or thanking God. It restores justice in the universe. From the very beginning, humans were created as peaceful creatures. Adam and Eve were fed in Eden without killing; more than vegetarians, they were fruitarians—only eating fruits and not destroying plants for sustenance. Of course, they ruined that original state by eating forbidden fruit, and were cursed with agriculture, having to earn their bread by the sweat of their brows. And humans continued to disobey, becoming so dreadful that God regretted having made them, and destroyed every person, except Noah and his family. After the flood, God promised not to do it again, but also he made a concession to human weakness and reportedly said, "Every creature that lives and moves shall be food for you; I give you them all, as once I gave you all green plants."[4] In other words, humans were allowed to eat anything they wanted. They could kill to eat.

But that very act of killing makes us unclean. And for it, God wants retribution in the form of punishment. It doesn't even matter who gets punished. For our iniquities, we can punish a goat instead, a scapegoat as it were, sacrificed on the altar. It may seem odd to modern ways of thinking, but this logic is purely "an eye for an eye." If someone kills or commits sin, someone or some animal must be punished. And when it is offered to God, the community once again becomes whole, and righteous. "And further, for your life blood I will demand satisfaction, from every animal I will require it, and from a man also I will require satisfaction for the death of his fellow man."[5] The sacrifice constitutes that satisfaction, and it absolves the sinner.

You are by now no doubt wondering what this has to do with sharing food. Think of what happens when a community witnesses this act of sacrifice. They suddenly realize that not only are they fragile individuals, but so is everyone around them, and taking a life must be something special and sacred, and of course animal. They begin to think not only about how other living beings are killed in order to sustain them, but how much they depend on the lives of others. Ultimately, it is a way to pacify the community internally, because killing is serious business and thus the act draws them together and does make them, in a real sense, righteous.

Needless to say, watching slaughter is not something most people do regularly anymore. And its absence has made us careless with life, so that we no longer atone for taking it. Meat comes in a plastic package, it has nothing to do with living animals. I think on this point I would agree with Jean-Jacques Rousseau who, to paraphrase, said fine, if you want to eat meat, go ahead, but be prepared to kill the animal yourself. "I mean with your own hands, without iron tools, without knives. Tear them apart with your nails, as do lions and bears. Bite this cow and rip him to pieces."[6] Rousseau was advocating vegetarianism, which I'm not doing here. I am merely saying that we should be more cognizant of what we do with animals, and killing or at least witnessing the act in all its gore should be a rite of passage that allows you to eat it. And, exactly as in these ancient sacrifices, the entire event should be celebratory. The animal should be divided up and shared with everyone. That is, incidentally, exactly what happens in the Muslim sacrifice for Eid al-Fitr. A goat or sheep is slaughtered ritually by thanking the animal, with its head facing Mecca, and in the name of Allah its throat is slit so as to be as painless as possible. The sacrifice is then divided up and shared with neighbors. My larger point is not that we should revive temple sacrifice, but I do think if we are to have a healthy or even righteous behavior toward animals, we need to think ritually about how and why we kill them.

Another aspect of the ritual feast worth mentioning is that during many such events, people would be drinking—wine in the case of the great ancient Greek communal sacrifices, and a lot of it when it was to honor Dionysus. The wine in this case is called an *entheogen*, a way to incorporate the god physically into your body, much the way the Christian Eucharist works, not coincidentally also with wine. But it can also be *soma* among the ancient Aryans, or peyote among Native Americans.

Think about what happens in a crowd when you start to get tipsy. You begin to do things you wouldn't, normally. You are less conscious of the physical space around you—it becomes all right for people to get closer than normal. You lose inhibitions, and get sucked into the group. Freud called this a universal feeling that can be brought on by drugs, or even by the natural chemical intoxicants our brain produces—the euphoria of endorphins, that act sort of like opiates. However it is brought on, the ritual draws us in to the group. This is not just by virtue of the fact that it's done regularly, or because everyone knows what's going to happen so it becomes a tradition, but because we become subsumed and part of a greater whole rather than a collection of individuals. We lose our sense of self. It's comparable to what happens to a sports team in the middle of a game, or people thrashing around slam dancing in a mosh pit. The experience is ecstatic (from the Latin *ex stasis*—out of your place) because you are lifted from your place and time, from your own body, and become part of the whole. Of course, the crowd mentality can lead people to do horrible things as well, but in this ritual form, it creates community and oneness with others. Such connections are essential for survival of a community and thus all societies create rituals, usually involving food and often drugs, which give people a sense of belonging within the unified group.

Another example of an act of sharing, a food ritual that creates community, is known as Carnival. This is the time preceding Lent in the Christian calendar. In earlier times, all remaining meat and dairy products had to be consumed during this period, before the forty-day fast. The word carnival has some connection to *carne* or meat. It is sometimes claimed that carne-vale means farewell to meat, but this makes no sense. The word *vale* in Latin means "be strong," not farewell. Regardless of the etymology, more important than what you eat is how you eat it. Carnival, also known as Fat Tuesday and Mardi Gras, is a day of ritual subversion. All the normal rules of society are turned upside down. You're allowed to get blind drunk, lift your shirt to passersby, rudely satirize public figures with parade floats—and that's only the mild version in New Orleans. In the middle ages, it was also time to openly mock your superiors with fake weddings, trials, even masses. Anything normally held sacred was ridiculed. While masked and anonymous, you could mock the lord of the manor, the village priest, anyone. Chiefly, it was a day of grotesque indulgence; people would stuff themselves silly. One person, usually the lowliest, would be crowned king for the day—and for this one day a year, everyone was equal. Note that everyone was ritually equal, not literally, since it was all a kind of play.

Historically, at the end of the festivities, a fat man armed with phallic sausages would tilt with a skinny figure impersonating Lent, armed with fish and vegetables, and of course Lent always had to win. Then everything would go back to exactly the way it was before. The regular order of society was not only restored but strengthened—because on this one day everyone got to blow off steam. I don't mean that in an informal way, to relax and not go to work, but in a very real psychological sense. Imagine your average peasant, who every day had to bow down in deference to his superiors. This was one day he could channel all his pent-up frustrations and mock those he served openly without fear of reprisal. The ritual thus acted as a safety valve.[7] And in the end, everyone pretended it never happened. The ritual thus built community and strengthened the order of society. It's only in the early modern period that real violence began to break out and the carnivals were all shut down, in Catholic and Protestant Europe.[8] (New Orleans's Mardi Gras is actually a nineteenth century revival; Venice's is more of a fashion show today.)

Carnival in its original form was not just a fun picnic held every year when people saw friends and relatives, though that was important. It was an act of sharing through ritual that bound the community together and expressed shared values through the medium of food. We really don't have many public food rituals anymore; church ales were moved into taverns and ale houses which could be taxed,[9] public processions and communal feasts held on saint's days diminished, as did public days of thanksgiving. Even raucous food fairs like Bartholomew Fair, where pork was celebrated in excess, were eventually suppressed in the eighteenth and nineteenth centuries. Since the mid-nineteenth century we have an official holiday for Thanksgiving, but it is very much a private family celebration, aligned with the kind of domestic ideal Victorian moralists were trying to foster in immigrants to make them behave and act like Americans.[10]

Even if you look at modern carnivals and state fairs, they are largely about eating and are in many ways subversive. You eat all sorts of garbage you wouldn't ordinarily: corn dogs and funnel cakes, deep fried candy bars and the like. But they are really not communal celebrations, they're a handful of private vendors that pull up in trucks and go from town to town. They are usually not local people. For example, there's a huge Asparagus Festival in Stockton every spring, and there is a local tent that does fried asparagus, but the vast majority of people selling food do it professionally and go from festival to festival across the country. Most food festivals are really about marketing a city, making money, and trying to invent a sense of place.

I think the closest thing we have to a subversive food ritual is the eating competition. Normally, we are expected to eat moderately, slowly, with utensils, and to be polite. But on this one occasion, we're encouraged to use our hands (or not when it comes to pies), and eat as much as possible as quickly as we can. The professional food competitions are amazing, but the local ones that involve people who live in the community are in a way more interesting, because the crowd knows the competitors, and there is a lot more at stake regarding local boasting rights because you are competing with people you know and will see again. But let's think about what is really going on in this ritual. It is akin to the medieval folk tale of *The Land of Cockaigne*—in Italian, *Cuccagna*; *Schlaraffenland* in German; *Luilekkerland* in Dutch.[11] In this place, people just wallow on the ground while food falls into their mouths, pies slide off roofs, cooked pigs run around with knives stuck in their backs, ready for slicing. There is a never-ending river of wine. There is never any work, and no one ever ages because there's a Fountain of Youth. It's always spring. There's also free love. The story is very much a peasant's dream; the food is simple and rustic, not exotic delicacies. What matters here is volume. In Boccaccio's *Decameron*, written in the 1350s, there is the Land of Bengodi, with a mountain of parmesan cheese, and people roll macaroni down it and into their mouths. The folk song "Big Rock Candy Mountain" is much the same, with rivers of whiskey and cigarette trees.

If you have ever seen the TV show *Man vs. Food*, it functions in much the same way.[12] An ordinary guy, Adam Richman, is challenged with a ridiculous amount of completely ordinary food—a huge pizza, a twenty-pound hamburger, a monster six-foot sandwich, or a huge pile of spicy wings. He tries to finish the whole thing in an allotted time period. Apart from being disgusting, it's also a fantasy of subversion. Viewers at one level imagine how sick he's going to get, but they're also thinking, What if I could break all the rules, eat as much as I wanted and never gain weight, never get sick, and just go from one pig-out session to another? Of course, the performance never encourages this kind of behavior, it does exactly the opposite. It reminds us that we don't want to be like this depraved sweaty beast. It gets us to follow communally sanctioned norms. Like all negative examples, it provides a moral lesson that encourages us to conform. In that respect, much like carnival, it strengthens the community, as does most satire. (I do believe the show is satire, though the audience doesn't always seem to understand that.) Richman is essentially the modern day Grobianus, a sixteenth century literary character who taught people manners through bad example, farting, belching, vomiting, and doing all sorts of disgusting things.[13] My larger point is that we *need* food competitions, grotesque displays of outrageous behavior, which I think do a much better job of getting people to eat well than government-sponsored nutrition programs, food pyramids, or healthy-eating ads.

Another way community is built through sharing food is when the sharing serves as a boundary marker, delineating who belongs to the group and who doesn't on the basis of foods that are ritually pure versus those that are taboo. It is often said that the kosher laws of the ancient Hebrews were essentially formed to differentiate them from people around them, like the Canaanites, who did eat pork and other forbidden foods. I think there is a much more complex logic to these rules, which mostly have to do with not eating carnivorous animals that kill (and don't appease with sacrifice and are therefore unclean). The rule about only eating animals that chew their cud and have a cloven hoof is a shorthand way of recognizing ruminants—which are always vegetarian and don't kill to eat. Anyway, the ancient Hebrews were very clearly also concerned about not losing their identity, hence rules about not marrying outside the faith, and not eating with people of other faiths—eating with someone is one step away from getting to know them and possibly knowing them too well.

You could also say that the Hindu food prohibitions serve a similar function. In this case, people of higher castes cannot accept food prepared by those of a lower caste. And the higher you go, the more complex the food prohibitions; Brahmins at the top are often purely vegetarian. Dietary codes here separate different kinds of people and keep them apart in an effort to maintain distinct status. I think even informal food rules serve a similar function today. There are people who won't eat certain foods as a rule, ostensibly for ethical reasons or to maintain a certain body shape, but the restrictions serve as a boundary marker, precisely the same way these ancient food codes function. It separates the individual or group as purer and holier than others who are less discriminating about what they eat.

There has been a great deal of scholarship lately about the performative nature of food as an expression of identity. Eating specific, emblematic foods publicly, so that your own group members (and also outsiders) witness it is a way of strengthening group cohesion. In my own city we have annual Greek and Jewish food festivals, among others. There are particular foods everyone expects at these events: baklava, gyros, and souvlaki at the former; latkes, blintzes, bagels, and lox at the latter. Even though people eat whatever they like at other times, this is a day to wear your ethnicity proudly and publicly. The same thing happens at family gatherings; a black family might eat traditional dishes, an Italian family might make only complex, handmade recipes handed down from *nonna*. Or a Mexican family could gather to make *tamales* by hand for a special feast. Notice that these occasions are usually holidays or special occasions; the tribe gathers together and reminds each other of who they are and where they came from through specially prepared foods—which are always the same. That is to say, once again: People perform identity with food, to themselves and others, much as they would do it with music, dance, costume, or language.

In this respect, just as food rules can be used as a boundary marker, sharing food with outsiders is an invitation to find common ground. It is hard to fight with someone once you have invited them into your home, broken bread together, and shared a glass of wine.

The modern ritual that seems closest to the kind of communal festival I'm discussing here is the potluck. These can be small events at one particular home, a church supper, a block party, a Fourth of July picnic, any time when each person is expected to bring a special dish and share it with others. As we all know, these often end up being competitive, at some level. People may be reluctant to bring store-bought food since the whole point is to show off your skills. Sometimes these are formally competitive as well—a chili cook-off, for example, or a barbecue competition. Setting aside the commercial competitions in which professionals arrive with their souped-up rigs, let's focus on the small-scale potluck where guests don't know each other. More than a chance to show off, this is also an opportunity to eat with new acquaintances—a neighbor down the block or a member of your church with whom you've never spoken. But it's very different than sitting down at a wedding or a common table at some event, because in those instances, everyone is eating professionally prepared food. At a potluck, you are actually physically ingesting the material resources and labor of someone else: a stranger, in fact. It involves a certain amount of trust. I am going so far as to eat your food, expecting (1) that you're not going to poison me, (2) that you actually know what you're doing in the kitchen, and (3) that you will extend to me the same form of trust. It is a kind of symbolic exchange. I am letting you partake in my sustenance while you partake in mine. Because there is a lot riding on the exchange, we are also very careful to be polite. We don't want to insult someone by grimacing or spitting it out, even if it is horrible. It is the one time when we will be absolutely and utterly civil, because we are equally vulnerable.

What happens when the exchange goes well? When you're offered a compliment? It is actually much more valuable and reassuring than coming from a good friend or relative. Because even though we know everyone will be polite, the stranger can in fact terminate the exchange at any moment. They might walk away in disinterest, or smile halfheartedly. Sometimes we have family members or friends who tell us the truth point blank, just to be honest, but often close friends fear insulting you, so they pass on pro forma compliments. With strangers, the compliment must be genuine, and so I would argue the satisfaction is much greater. I recently had this exact experience when a total stranger came up to me at a potluck party and said, "Wow, did you make that?!"

Allow me to parse exactly where the pleasure of cooking for others lies. This may sound counterintuitive, but I think the prime motivation for people to do anything is not profit. Profit is merely a means to other things—buying material objects, security, whatever. As social beings, what we really crave is the approval of others, recognition for a job well done. We even secretly enjoy the envy of others. It is perhaps only in a capitalist economy that we immediately confuse this kind of approval with material wealth. Properly, it should be for the work that goes into it. Sometimes people even tend to think that if you can get rich doing something bad, it's still admirable. But at its root, social capital and estimation really come from personal accomplishment, having made good things, brought favorable situations into being, having acquired a certain expert skill or knowledge. This holds true for any profession. We admire the great athlete despite the millions they make, we value the physician for sleuthing out a diagnosis, or the lawyer for arguing brilliantly, or the actor for bringing the house down. In each case, the prime value of the act is in the applause.

This is equally true for cooking, whether it's a professional chef in a high-end restaurant or a parent making a routine meal, whether it garners a great review in the *Times* and three Michelin stars or a fleeting nod of approval. I would go further, that over and above other accomplishments, sharing of food is deeper and more fundamental—because it is a requirement. Like all basic biological functions, it is not at the periphery but at the core of our being, as is physical or mental prowess, and reproduction. These are the things we absolutely need for survival, so they are more directly hardwired into our pleasure receptors. They are instinctual; just as a mother bird feeds her chicks, or a bear provides for her cubs, the act of sharing food is a central part of what it means to be human. This extends beyond our children to our immediate clan, our larger tribe and, for the socially conscious, to everyone—our entire nation and everyone on the planet. The pleasure receptors in our brains fire when food is well shared. In this case I think it is different from other forms of altruism. You might think, cynically, that doing good for others is essentially a calculation that they will return the favor, but I don't think so. We do it without any expectation of return; we do it because we need to.

So what effect does this have on us when an increasing number of meals are eaten in solitude, on the run, in the car, at one's desk? These are the demands of modern life. We are too busy, because there are more important things to do than eat. I think it destroys something that is absolutely required for our survival. And I would say that even though it's perhaps difficult to arrange or even unpleasant, the family meal is a necessity. The communal feast is required for fully developed social interaction. Eating with and sharing food with kin or friends is an absolute prerequisite of cohesion and viability, and indeed of happiness.

Dessert

How do the several parts of these chapters fit together? Obviously they are sequential: you have to grow the food before you process or cook it, and only then can you share it. But I would also say that if any one part is missing, the entire social and cultural meaning of eating is in danger of being lost. It threatens to become mere feeding—maintenance of the human machine and nothing more. We might as well be lined up at a trough or take food in pill form. By necessity in the past, farming, cooking, and eating took place in one and the same location or at least in close proximity within one community. All three parts of human nourishment need to be as close as possible. We should know the people who are involved in making what we eat. We can't begin to think about health or happiness provided by food without thinking seriously about the impact of our farming practices, the nasty additives that go into our food to perk up flavor or extend shelf life, or the other indignities that are sold to people and purport to be nourishing. Food will cease to have any meaning whatsoever when we lose our ability to discern good from bad, flavorful from artificial, healthy food from junk.

Wellcome Library, London

Cordial

To close this book, I thought I'd offer you a wee nip of something strong, to aid the digestion and comfort the heart. Or rather, show you how to do it, so you can enjoy the whole process. It takes a great deal of patience and perseverance, but is well worth it.

It helps if you live somewhere really hot like I do, but I know there are many places around the country where grapes thrive. Use whatever grows in your area, preferably *vinifera*, but even concord grapes work well. Start by taking a cutting from a grape vine in the fall during harvest season. A foot or two will be fine. You can also buy a plant, of course, but this is more fun. Wrap it in newspaper and keep wet until the spring. Stick it in the ground in a sunny spot facing south, with good drainage. Poor soil is perfectly fine. If you like, tie it to a stake to help it stay straight. It will bud, bear leaves, and grow vigorously. It may take a few years, but eventually you will have a sturdy vine that will bear grapes. Plant as many as you like. Let them ramble up a pergola or trellis, too; their tendrils know where to grab.

In the fall, collect your grapes, without leaves or stems, and put them in a big, clean bucket. Don't use antibacterial soap in the bucket. And don't be tempted to wash the grapes. The powdery stuff on the grapes is yeast. Crush them well, however you like, and leave the bucket open, but cover it with cheesecloth to keep out fruit flies. Twice a day, push down the floating skin and seeds. Eventually it will start bubbling and smelling like wine. Yes, it is that easy. After about two weeks, drain off the liquid and squeeze out the remaining juice from the skins and seeds. I do this in a sturdy, clean dishtowel in many successive batches. By twisting it, you'll get most of the juice out. Don't worry if it's cloudy, we're not going for clarity here. Taste it if you like—very young, fresh wine can be delightful.

Put it in a closed vessel and let it settle for a few days. Then pour it into a still, leaving behind any mucky dregs. If you don't have a still, a glass retort flask bought at a chemistry supply shop works well too. The size all depends on how much you want to make. I usually do three liters at a time, in two batches, because that's about how much wine I usually get each year. Heat the wine in the still up to about 90 degrees Celsius, which will allow the alcohol to vaporize but not the water. It will course up the tube and then condense back into liquid in the "snake" of the still. At this point, you will get maybe a full bottle of clear, potent hooch. You can consume it right then, or let it age. A wooden barrel would be ideal, but a few oak chips in the bottle actually do the trick also.

When it is golden, pour some for a friend and sip slowly. This is contentment.

Notes

First Course

1. Richard J. Dalik, *Manalapan and Englishtown* (Mt. Pleasant, SC: Arcadia Publishing, 1997).

2. Janice Kohl Sarapin, *Old Burial Grounds of New Jersey: A Guide.* (New Brunswick: Rutgers University Press, 1994).

3. Lisa Laird, *Applejack: The Spirit of Americana* (Scobeyville, NJ: Laird, 1992). See also the chapter on apples in Michael Pollan, *The Botany of Desire* (NewYork: Random House, 2002).

4. Cato The Elder, *On Farming*, translated by Andrew Dalby (Totnes: Prospect Books, 1998); *Petri de Crescentiis, Opus Ruralium Commodorum*, manuscript facsimile (Vicenza: Biblioteca Internationale "La Vigna," 2010); Vincenzo Tanara, *L'Economia Del Cittadino in Villa* (Venice: Stefano Curti, 1674), available in reprint from the University of Michigan Library www.lib.umich.edu and the first 1651 edition on Google books, along with many other editions, for free.

5. Mauro Ambrosoli, *The Wild and the Sown: Botany and Agriculture in Western Europe 1350-1850* (Cambridge: Cambridge University Press, 1997).

6. Slicher van Bath, *The Agrarian History of Western Europe: 500-1850* (London: Edward Arnold, 1963); Marcel Mazoyer and Laurence Roudart, *A History of World Agriculture from the Neolithic Age to the Current Crisis*, translated by James H. Membrez (NewYork: Monthly Review Press, 2006).

7. See for example *The Community Land Trust: A Guide to a New Model of Land Tenure in America* by the International Independence Institute, 1972.

8. Tanara, *L'Economia Del Cittadino in Villa*, 141.

9. Ibid., 193.

10. Ibid., 169, 170.

11. Bartolomeo Stefani, *L'Arte di ben cucinare* (Mantua: Osanna, 1662. Reprint Bologna: Arnaldo Forni, 2000), 61.

12. Ibid., 266.

13. Thomas More, *Utopia*, translated by Peter K. Marshall (New York: Washington Square Press, 1965), Book II, Chapter 1.

Second Course

1. See the NPD Group's "National Eating Trends" data collected over the past 30 years.

2. "Profiling Food Consumption in America," http://www.usda.gov/factbook/chapter2.pdf

3. United States Department of Labor-Bureau of Labor Statistics, American Time Use Survey, http://www.bls.gov/tus/current/eating.htm

4. Food safety regulation is a huge topic. Two very useful accounts are Suzanne Freidberg, *Fresh: A Perishable History* (Cambridge: Belknap Press of Harvard University Press, 2010) and Harvey Levenstein, *Fear of Food* (Chicago: University of Chicago Press, 2012).

5. Nancy Silverton, *Breads from La Brea Bakery: Recipes for the Connoisseur* (New York: Villard Press, 1996); Peter Reinhardt's *Artisan Breads Every Day* (Berkeley: Ten Speed Press, 2009).

6. Gervase Markharm. *The English Housewife*, ed. Michael R. Best (Montreal and Kingston: McGill-Queens University Press, 1986).

7. Bartolomeo Scappi. *Opera*, translated by Terence Scully (Toronto: University of Toronto Press, 2008).

8. Christoforo di Messisbugo, *Banchetti* (Ferrara: Buglhat and Hucher, 1549), 103.

9. The best article I have seen explaining this is Joseph G. Sebranek and James N. Bacus, "Cured meat products without the addition of nitrate or nitrite: what are the issues?" *Meat Science* 77, 2007, 136-147. Available online at http://www.vet.unipi.it/system/files/Cured%20meat%20products%20without%20direct%20addition%20of%20nitrate%20or%20nitrite.pdf

10. Pantalone da Confienza, *Summa Lacticiniorum* (Turin, 1477); Jacob Bifrons, in Jodoco Willich (Conrad Gesner) *Ars magirica* (Zurich: Jacob Gesner, 1563).

11. Guilio Landi (pseudonym), *Formaggiata di Sere Stentato* (Piacenza: Grassino Formaggiaro, 1542). Online at http://books.google. com/books?id=lCM6AAAAcAAJ&printsec=frontcover&source=g bs_ge_summary_r&cad=0#v=onepage&q&f=false

12. Agostino Gallo, *Le vinti giornata di agricultura* (First edition, 1564; Venice: Borgomineri Fratelli, 1572).

13. Josiah Twamley, *Dairying Exemplified or The Business of Cheesemaking* (Warwick: J. Sharp, 1784).

Third Course

1. Richard Wrangham, *Catching Fire: How Cooking Made Us Human* (New York: Basic Books, 2009).

2. Juvenal, *The Satires of Juvenal*, translated by Rolfe Humphries (Bloomington: Indiana University Press, 1958).

3. The Book of Leviticus is the best source for details about ancient Hebrew Temple sacrifice, and the various forms it can take, including grain, cakes without leaven, and so forth.

4. Genesis 6.

5. Genesis 9:5.

6. Jean-Jacques Rousseau, *Emile*, translated by Allan Bloom (New York: Basic Books, 1979), 155.

7. Mikhail Bakhtin, *Rabelais and His World*, translated by Helene Iswolsky (Bloomington: Indiana University Press, 2009).

8. Peter Burke, *Popular Culture in Early Modern Europe* (New York: Harper and Row, 1978).

9. Bennett, Judith M., *Ale, Beer, and Brewsters in England: Women's Work in a Changing World, 1300-1600.* (New York: Oxford University Press, 1996).

10. Andrew F. Smith, *Turkey: An American Story.* (Urbana: University of Illinois Press, 2006).

11. Herman Pleij, *Dreaming of Cockaigne* (New York: Columbia University Press, 2001).

12. http://www.travelchannel.com/tv-shows/man-v-food

13, Frederick Dedekind, *Grobianus et Grobiana: sive, de morum simplicitate, libri tres* (Cologne, 1558). Also on line at http://books.google.com/books?id=BrqVlSIoJgoC&printsec=frontcover&source=gbs_ge_summary_r&cad=0#v=onepage&q&f=false. English version translated by R.F. (Gent), *The Schoole of Slovenrie: Or, Cato Turnd* (sic) *Wrong Side Outward* (Valentine Simmes, 1605).

Index